# THE Qi OF Personal Finance AND Investing

## *A Heretic's Guide*

**FRANK SEINSHEIMER III, M.D.**

© Seinsheimer III, M.D. 2020

ISBN: 978-1-09835-049-9

eBook ISBN: 978-1-09835-050-5

All rights reserved. This book or any portion thereof may not be reproduced or used in any manner whatsoever without the express written permission of the publisher except for the use of brief quotations in a book review.

Learn from everyone
Question everything
Decide for yourself
Become your own teacher

Definition:
Qi: The force that makes up and binds together all things in the universe; the vital life force that flows through the body.

# ACKNOWLEDGEMENTS

Once again, I wish to thank my wife and family for their love, strength and support these many years. Thanks are also due to my many teachers, mentors and colleagues in various fields over uncounted years who helped and instructed me while tolerating my frequent challenges, questioning and skepticism. Another callout to my wife, Lynne, for her love and toleration of me. Our 50+ years together have been precious, treasured and lucky. Thanks also to Lynne and Steve Leighton, an old Yale friend, for their thoughtful criticism and suggestions when this book was in manuscript form.

# THE AUTHOR

Frank Seinsheimer III, M.D. is a graduate of Walnut Hills High School, Yale University and Harvard Medical School. He trained in General Surgery at the Peter Bent Brigham Hospital, in Orthopedic Surgery at the Harvard Combined Orthopedic Residency Program at the Massachusetts General Hospital and in Hand Surgery at the Thomas Jefferson University Hospital. He spent 37 ½ years in the private practice of Hand Surgery and Orthopedic Surgery in Montgomery County, Maryland. Frank Seinsheimer III has trained for over thirty years in martial arts and has black belts in Tae Kwon Do, Aikido and Japanese Jujitsu. He took all of the investment, finance and economics courses in the flexible MBA program at the Johns Hopkins University. He was a fiduciary for the profit sharing program for his orthopedic group for 35 years.

Dr. Seinsheimer has read extensively in finance and investing literature and has spent decades studying, understanding and finally disagreeing with the basic theory underlying the decisions of the financial world. He has reached conclusions regarding personal finance and investing which are distinctly different and heretical from the standard advice given by most financial advisors and financial managers. His fourth book, "The Qi of Personal Finance and Investing: A Heretic's Guide", contains his thoughts, opinions and advice regarding personal finance and investing.

Dr. Seinsheimer has written three other books. The first, "Unarmed Defense Against Weapons", covers the subject of realistic streetwise martial arts with emphasis on how to defend yourself against an attack by an armed assailant. The second, "Poetical Commentary", contains poems, many of which are commentary about life, the universe and everything. The third, "The Qi of the Scalpel" is a medical memoir which covers his medical training and post graduate years of practice.

# TABLE OF CONTENTS

**The Author** ............................................................................................. iii

**Preface** .................................................................................................. vii

**Chapter One:**
    *Risk: What is risk?* ............................................................................ 1

**Chapter Two**
    *Exponential Growth vs. Linear Growth; Compounding* ............................ 7

**Chapter Three:**
    *Some Common Investing and Financial Terms* .................................... 12

**Chapter Four:**
    *The Psychology of Investing* ............................................................ 19

**Chapter Five:**
    *Who Can You Trust?* ...................................................................... 29

**Chapter Six:**
    *Risk Revisited; Inflation Revisited; Safety Revisited* ............................ 42

**Chapter Seven:**
    *The Cost of Investing* ..................................................................... 48

**Chapter Eight:**
    *Other Investment Risks* .................................................................. 63

**Chapter Nine:**
    *My Critique of Modern Portfolio Theory* ............................................ 79

**Chapter Ten:**
    *Diversification* ............................................................................. 116

**Chapter Eleven:**
    *Rebalancing* ................................................................................ 123

**Chapter Twelve:**
*Borrowing* ........................................................................................... 128

**Chapter Thirteen**
*Choosing a financial advisor or financial manager ….. OR NOT!* ........... 141

**Chapter Fourteen:**
*Retirement* ......................................................................................... 145

**Chapter Fifteen:**
*Predicting the Future* ......................................................................... 155

**Chapter Sixteen:**
*Further Discussion Regarding Predicting the Future* ......................... 156

**Chapter Seventeen:**
*Reprise* ............................................................................................... 166

**Chapter Eighteen:**
*Precis* ................................................................................................. 170

**Chapter Nineteen:**
*The End: The Conclusion; The Summation: Finis* ............................. 171

# PREFACE

First:

Most people feel that the subjects of personal finance, investments and generally the whole financial world are too complicated for them to understand.

**NOT TRUE; NOT TRUE; NOT TRUE**

This book differs from other personal finance and investing books in a number of crucial aspects.

Because in this book:

I explain why:

**USING FINANCIAL MANAGERS ACTUALLY HARMS YOUR LONG TERM INVESTING RESULTS!**

I explain why:

**FOLLOWING THE ADVICE OF MOST FINANCIAL ADVISORS HARMS YOUR LONG TERM INVESTING RESULTS!**

I explain why:

**FOLLOWING THE CURRENT INVESTING THEORY (MODERN PORTFOLIO THEORY) HARMS YOUR LONG TERM INVESTING RESULTS!**

I explain why:

**THE FAILURE TO MINIMIZE YOUR YEARLY COST OF INVESTING HARMS YOUR LONG TERM INVESTING RESULTS!**

I explain why:

**EXCESSIVE DIVERSIFICATION HARMS YOUR LONG TERM INVESTING RESULTS!**

I explain why:

**UNDERSTANDING RISK, INFLATION AND EXPONENTIAL GROWTH ARE NECESSARY FOR YOUR FINANCIAL LITERACY!**

I explain why:

**IT IS IMPORTANT TO LEARN ENOUGH ABOUT PERSONAL FINANCE AND INVESTING TO BECOME YOUR OWN TEACHER!**

I explain why:

**YOU NEED TO BE CAREFUL WHO YOU TRUST WITH YOUR MONEY!**

I explain why:

**YOU NEED DISCIPLINE IN YOUR SPENDING BEHAVIOR!**

I explain why:

# Preface

**I CONSIDER MYSELF THE PACHYDERM IN THE PARLOR OF PERSONAL FINANCE AND INVESTING!**

I explain why:

**MY OPINIONS AND ADVICE REGARDING PERSONAL FINANCE AND INVESTING ARE HERETICAL!**

Enough of the "I explain why's".

Let's move on.

In this book I present a simple and effective method for successful long term investing. Note, please, my emphasis on long term. I will explain in simple terms why I believe that the basic theory (Modern Portfolio Theory) used by most financial advisors and financial managers is flawed. I will discuss why I believe following this theory results in sub-optimal investing results. I will explain why I believe that the basic theory underpinning all of the financial advice you hear and all of the financial management you receive will actually harm your long term investing results.

There! I have set myself a high bar to clear. I have declared myself a heretic.

I have found through past experience that financial advisors and managers seem to deliberately present their advice in a complicated manner. I believe that they do this to intimidate their prospective clients. I believe that they do this to make the clients feel that they, the clients, desperately need the advice and management of their financial advisors and financial managers. As you read this book, you will understand why I recommend against the use of financial advisors and financial managers who charge a percentage of your invested assets each year.

Second:
Why am I writing this book? The lack of "financial literacy" in the general population is huge! My purpose in this book is to provide an understandable approach to financial literacy.

What is financial literacy?

Definition:
"Financial literacy is the possession of the set of skills and knowledge that allows an individual to make informed and effective decisions with all of their financial resources." (Wikipedia, September 18, 2020)

Note:
Many of my references to other sources will be to Wikipedia. This open, free online encyclopedia is available to any and to all for free. The entries in Wikipedia may be changed at any time by the Wikipedia editors. Thus, my references to Wikipedia will give the date I went online to Wikipedia for the information or the quote. Similarly, my references to other websites, which are also subject to change, will include the date I obtained the quote online.

Back to financial literacy.

This book is all about your (the reader's) financial literacy. I will cover issues like saving, investing, who you can trust, who you should not trust, buying a car, buying a house, why you should not use a financial manager who charges a percentage of your investment each year, why you need to keep your yearly cost of investing low and last and most important why you need to become your own financial manager.

I discuss how you should take control and manage your own money and investments. I discuss how you should understand the "keep it simple stupid" basics of our seemingly complex financial world. I discuss in detail the difference between what seems risky and but is actually relatively safe in the investment universe. I discuss in detail the difference between what seems safe but is actually risky in the investment universe. My opinions regarding risk in investing are "heretical." Issues concerning risk and uncertainty pervade our lives and our financial decisions. I discuss and explain these issues in sufficient detail that you will be able to understand them. This is crucial to making sound financial decisions.

I believe that most financial advisors and financial managers calculate the "risk" of your basket of investments incorrectly! I explain why I believe this. I explain why I believe calculating the "risk" of your investing incorrectly harms your long term investing results. I discuss my heretical opinions regarding what I consider to be the major flaws in the financial advice and financial management provided by most financial advisors, financial managers and financial firms.

Financial literacy is vitally important to your future. Distinguishing between what is actually relatively safe and what is much riskier than it seems is the crux of my argument in this book. This book is designed to improve your financial literacy. This book does not attempt to cover all aspects of your financial life in encyclopedic fashion. This book does not discuss issues like how to get out of credit card debt.

This book is oriented more toward advising you why it is important to start saving money when you are young.

This book is oriented more toward advising you what to do once you start to save some money.

This book is oriented more toward advising you how to invest wisely.

Consider this book your introduction to becoming financially literate.

Consider this book the beginning of your financial education not the end.

Third:

Before I write anything else, let me assure you that there is no math in this book. There are no graphs in this book. I explain everything in terms that someone suffering from arithmophobia or numerophobia is able to comfortably understand. Arithmophobia and numerophobia are real words describing people with fear and anxiety regarding numbers and math.

Fourth:

Not another money book! This one is not written by a popular financial guru but by a common-sense practical guy. I am an orthopedic surgeon, a hand surgeon and I have black belts in three martial arts, tae kwon do, aikido and Japanese jujitsu. I also teach my version of martial arts, "Unarmed Defense Against Weapons." I am not a professional financial advisor. I am not a financial manager trying to drum up new clients. I am not a popular, modern media, financial personality desperate for viewer ratings.

Many years ago, when I became a partner in my orthopedic group, I realized that I was a fiduciary for the profit sharing plan which covered all of our employees including myself.

Definition:

A fiduciary is a person who holds a legal or ethical relationship of trust with one or more other parties (person or group of persons). Typically, a fiduciary takes care of money or assets for another person." (Wikipedia, August 21, 2020)

Recognizing my responsibility to my employees and also desiring best investing results for myself, I realized that I had little idea why our financial advisors and financial managers were telling us what they were telling us. I had little idea why they were making the decisions, they were making for us for the investments in our profit sharing plan.

Let me restate that.

It wasn't that I had little idea why they were saying what they were saying and why they were managing our money the way they were managing our money. Actually, I had NO idea whatsoever. To be trite, I realized that I was truly clueless.

I wanted to understand the who, what, why, when and where of personal finance and investing.

I do not like being ignorant regarding a topic important to my life. I wanted to understand what the hidden gears beneath the financial industry surface were doing. I am an avowed sceptic. I wanted to understand the motivations of our financial advisors and managers. Actually, I wanted to understand the motivations of ALL financial advisors and ALL financial managers.

I began extensive reading regarding finance and investing. I took most of the finance, economics and investment courses in the Masters in Business Administration (MBA) extension program of Johns Hopkins University in the evening. I skipped the marketing courses. I did not see a personal need for the other courses and felt no reason to continue to obtain the MBA degree.

Fifth:

I consider myself a practical idealist. As stated above, I am also a devoted sceptic. One of my personal mantras is, "**What works?**" I studied the theories, the data and the accepted gospel, tenets and faith of the financial industry. I received the grade of A in all of my courses. As a committed sceptic, I continually questioned:

"What works?"

"What is real?"

"What should I truly believe?"

"What should I truly disbelieve?"

**Figuring out what to disbelieve is often more important than figuring out what to believe.**

Here is where the motto I inserted at the beginning of this book becomes pertinent.

I repeat:

Learn from everyone

Question everything

Decide for yourself

Become your own teacher

In my study of finance and investing, I have followed this motto.

In this book, I shall try to move you through the steps of this motto until you reach the point of becoming your own teacher when it concerns personal finance and investing.

If you read this book you will find that I am quite the heretic when it comes to the financial industry. Most members of the financial industry follow the religion of "Modern Portfolio Theory." (more, much more on this later) I have disavowed the common herd mentality of the financial industry. I disagree with the basic assumption of Modern Portfolio Theory. I explain why later in this book. If the basic assumption of Modern Portfolio Theory is "wrong" then all of the results, all of the decisions, all of the advice and all of the money management decisions that follow the use of Modern Portfolio Theory will lead to suboptimal results.

Sixth:

**There is real risk that many people today will not reach the level of financial security they desire before they reach retirement age. This book is designed to address that risk.**

Seventh:

From my point of view, rare, unpredictable, extreme events, sometimes referred to as "black swans" (Wikipedia, August 15, 2020) seem to occur with surprisingly common frequency. For example, think of how often you hear there has been a 100 year storm event. It seems to me that I hear about it happening somewhere every year. This makes sense if you realize that there are far more than 100 places on earth where storms may occur. I think that "uncommon" events (black swans) occur so often because there are so many different ways in which isolated, individual, rare, unpredictable, extreme events may occur.

Eighth:

In Chapter 3, I discuss the meaning of many words and concepts used by financial advisors and financial managers and others in the investing community. These "words" include risk, uncertainty, stocks, bonds, mutual funds, exchange traded funds and annuities among others. If these terms are familiar to you, feel free to skip that chapter. If you work in the financial world, you may wish to skip to Chapters 7, 8 and 9. In Chapter 9 my heresy is in full war cry.

I wish to point out that the terms "risk" and "uncertainty" may be used differently by various authors. I tend to use "risk" and "uncertainty" somewhat interchangeably. I tend to emphasize the uncertainty which accompanies the risk of multiple possible outcomes, both good and bad. I have seen "risk" used to refer to probabilities when there is sufficient data for statistical calculations. I have seen "uncertainty" applied to unknown outcomes when there is insufficient data to calculate probabilities using statistics. This later use of terms may be economic terminology. I will stick with my use which I think is more common among non-professionals.

Ninth:
You will find that I frequently repeat myself in this book. I do this for three reasons. One: for emphasis. Two: for your education; we do not learn from hearing or reading something once. Three: the need for similar discussions arises in different contexts within this book and therefore I often repeat them. Four: Repetition helps learning. That was four reasons. I guess I can't count.

Tenth:
The purpose of this book is to educate you in financial literacy so that you will feel comfortable making your own financial decisions. Becoming financially literate is important if you wish to reach your long term financial independence goals. Becoming financially comfortable will play a major role in your happiness and security later in life.

# CHAPTER ONE:
# Risk: What is risk?

The Cambridge Dictionary defines risk as:

> "the possibility of something bad happening."

Why start a book about personal finance and investing with a discussion of risk?

For many people their biggest fear regarding risk is fear of loss! For many people the fear of loss dominates their investment decisions. Most people do not really understand risk. We are never taught about risk and uncertainty in our formal education. In this book I discuss risk as it relates to investment decisions. Successful investing requires an understanding that what may seem risky is not. Successful investing also requires an understanding that what does not seem risky may, in fact, be risky.

There are risks for which probabilities can be calculated due to the existence of a large enough amount of data that allows the use of statistics. There are risks which are sufficiently rare that no statistical calculation of probabilities is possible. Often, people assume that they are able to calculate risks in situations in which it is not possible to calculate the risks. The math that follows this false assumption may give results which appear to be correct. The math that follows this false assumption may be brilliant. However, the act of making the false assumption that the risk can be calculated will inevitably lead to results which do not reflect reality. Decisions based on calculations which are based on incorrect assumptions will be faulty.

In this book I discuss the issue of which assumptions, which facts and which calculations of investment risk are reliable and true. I also discuss which calculations of investment risk are not reliable or true. Since the fear of loss is central to our investment decisions, it is important to understand what we can really know. It is equally important that we understand what we can never know. This knowledge is central to successful decision making.

To some degree the question of risk is involved in almost everything we do, all of the time, everywhere and with everyone. You prepare a meal for yourself or your family. Is the food fresh? What are the chances of food poisoning? Are the mushrooms safe? Could they be poisonous? You travel to work. What are the chances of injury from an automobile or bus accident, a commuter train derailment, or a mugging to mention just a few possibilities? What are the risks of another large asteroid collision with Earth which happened over sixty million years ago? You are about to go out on a date with another person. How well do you know that person? Is it safe to go out with your date?

Most of these risks are "routine." That is, these risks occur daily, continuously, all of the time. They hover to some degree in the back of our minds. They are part of our ordinary everyday living. They are not in the front of our immediate consciousness. These everyday risks fade into the background of our lives. The concept of risk and our handling of risk is an integral part of who we are, what we are and how we live.

You are trying to decide whether to invest some of your money. What is your risk of loss if you make this investment? What is the possibility of gain if you make this investment? What is your risk of loss or gain if you make some other investment? What is your risk of loss if you chose to avoid any investment?

How we understand risk and how we handle risk pervades our lives. Deciding where you wish to live includes concerns about safety. Deciding what work, you wish to perform, includes concerns about safety. In the midst of this pandemic, doctors who have treated patients with the virus have contracted the illness and died. Deciding what car, you buy may include concerns about safety. Deciding to go up to the new date's apartment also includes concerns about safety. Our understanding or lack of understanding of risk also influences how we handle money and how we engage in investment and personal finance!

I ask again: What is risk?

I repeat:

At its simplest, the Cambridge Dictionary defines risk as:

> "the possibility of something bad happening."

Underlying the "possibility of something bad happening" is uncertainty. Uncertainty regarding whether that "something bad" will happen or not. Uncertainty of when that "something bad" may happen or not. From my personal point of view "risk" and "uncertainty" also include the possibility of something "good" happening. The uncertainty is not binary. That is, it is not necessarily a choice between A: a specific good happening and B: a specific bad happening. There is an entire continuum of possible happenings of varying degrees of "good" and "bad" which may or may not happen over an extended period of time within your lifetime and extending beyond your lifetime, if you think of your descendants.

I am writing this book during the pandemic of 2020. The pandemic of 2020 is an excellent example of uncertainty and risk. Prior to the recent pandemic, many people were aware of the severe flu pandemic of the second decade of the twentieth century. Prior to the recent pandemic many people were aware of the more recent SARS, MERS and H1N1virus disease outbreaks. Thus we, meaning everyone, knew intellectually that there was a risk of another severe pandemic, but we, meaning everyone, knew we hadn't experienced a severe pandemic for over a century. More than a century, more than three to four generations had passed since the occurrence of a severe pandemic. We knew that we were living in the era of modern medicine. We were "psychologically sure" that a pandemic couldn't, that a pandemic wouldn't happen in our lifetime. That is, everyone except perhaps for a few virus epidemiologists. Despite this awareness in the back of our minds of the risk of a new, severe pandemic, few if any of us acted to prepare for such a risk.

The Wikipedia entry for risk on July 30, 2020 included the statement: "The international standard definition of risk for common understanding in different applications is 'effect of uncertainty on objectives.'" If you had difficulty wrapping your brain around that sentence, so did I.

What I wish to point out is the emphasis in that definition of "risk" on "uncertainty". The Wikipedia entry also included a list of types of risk including: business risk, economic risk, environmental risk, financial risk, health, safety and environmental risks, information technology risk, insurance risk, occupational risk, project risk, safety risk and security risk. It is enough to make your head swim.

When events occur commonly, measuring the risk seems relatively easy. Thus, insurance companies exert tremendous effort to quantitate the risk that a 47-year-old man or a 65-year-old woman will die of a heart attack within a year. That data is numerous, available and measurable. When events occur commonly, it is easy to document and calculate the statistics regarding the uncertainty regarding the occurrence of that specific risk.

Yet even those carefully calculated risks are uncertain due to the possibility of severe "black swan" events such as the current pandemic. Even if insurance companies calculated for the possibility of a severe pandemic, there was no way for them to know it would occur in 2020. It is unlikely they carefully and fully predicted and planned for the government mandated lock downs and the resulting economic distress.

When events are uncommon such as the occurrence of a pandemic, quantitating risks is difficult or to be truthful essentially impossible. There is a strong tendency to think you can measure and thereby predict risk. Believing you can measure and predict risk makes us feel better. People, i.e. you and I, do not like uncertainty. We desperately do not like uncertainty. We play games with ourselves to deny to ourselves how much uncertainty exists in our lives. The rarity of the occurrence of unusual events makes it truly impossible to determine the validity of any calculation of uncertainty or risk that such an unusual event will occur within a specific time frame.

Most of us have fear and anxiety with respect to certain risks. For example, you have little fear and anxiety that the grocery store may be out of apples. Even if the grocery store is out of apples, that will not seriously impact your life. Whereas you may have excessive fear and anxiety regarding the risk of a shark attack when considering whether to swim in the ocean even though the risk is numerically low.

Many people are risk averse. That is, they fear bad outcomes and will act to avoid bad outcomes even if this behavior results in a lower probability of a good outcome. This has been measured in numerous ways in psychological experiments. With respect to finance, many people fear "loss." This fear of "loss" may lead to decisions which negatively affect investment results. Strong emotions tend to influence many of our behaviors. Money elicits strong emotions in most of us and often interferes with our logical decision making.

I will discuss the concept of "risk" as it involves finance and investment in much more detail later in this book. I will discuss current attempts to measure and quantitate risk as it pertains to investments. I believe that the current "methods of measuring investment risk" are faulty. I believe that the current methods of measuring the risk of investing in a basket of assets starts with a false assumption. I believe that using these incorrect "methods of measuring investment risk" leads to incorrect investment decisions by many financial advisors and financial managers. I discuss my reasoning later in this book.

What is the risk of buying a share of Apple and selling it within one hour, one day, one week, one year, twenty years or fifty years? What is the risk of buying shares in a low cost United States stock index fund and holding these shares for one hour, one day, one week, one year, twenty years or fifty years? What is the risk of buying a 50 year bond today and holding it for one hour, one day, one week, one year, twenty years or fifty years? The risks of each of these possibilities is quite different and for you probably unexpected. This book will help you think about the risks of these different possible investments in a knowledgeable manner.

Consider this chapter merely an introduction to the concepts of risk and uncertainty with respect to investing and finance.

CHAPTER TWO

# Exponential Growth vs. Linear Growth; Compounding

Why discuss concepts like exponential growth, linear growth and compounding early in this book?

Knowledge of exponential growth, linear growth and compounding is crucial to understanding successful investing.

You may find it rewarding to read and reread this chapter until you are satisfied you understand the concepts of exponential growth, linear growth and compounding.

I have promised to minimize the use of math in this book. I shall endeavor to keep that promise. I wish to make my discussion understandable to everyone who reads this book. There are a few mathematical concepts which are necessary to understanding finance and investing.

You do not have to be able to do the math.

I repeat:

You do not have to be able to do the math.

However, a general understanding of some mathematical concepts in important.

**What is the difference between linear growth and exponential growth? What is compounding?**

The answer to these questions is important in any discussion of personal finance and investing.

**Linear growth graphs as a straight line.**

A comparison of your age with the number of calendar years you have been alive is an example of linear growth. Each year your age increases by one year. The rate at which your age increases stays the same, namely one year of age per one calendar year. Similarly, if you compare your age in years with the number of months you have been alive or your age in months with the number of years you have been alive, these relationships will also graph as a straight line. Each year your age increases, twelve months have passed. The only difference between these relationships (age in years vs. calendar years passed; age in years vs. calendar months passed; age in months vs calendar years passed) is that the straight line graphs for one relationship will be steeper than another or shallower depending on the direction of your comparison.

I repeat:

If you graph your age on the upright or Y axis and the calendar year on the horizontal or X-axis, you get a straight line rising upwards as you move to the right. This is linear growth. If you graph your age in number of months, the graphed line will again be straight. The line will again rise as you move to the right. The rise will be steeper or shallower than the first example depending on how you choose your units of time or units of age. The relationship still graphs as a straight line. This is linear growth.

**Exponential growth increases in a steadily increasing manner.**

After a period of time, the rate of growth is faster than at the start. Sometime later the rate of growth is even faster. In exponential growth, a graphed line moves upward with time and rises faster and faster as you move to the right.

Rats breed exponentially in an ideal environment. A breeding pair of rats may have up to six litters per year and five to ten pups per litter. Rats reach maturity after nine weeks. So, a breeding pair of two rats may have ten pups in their first litter. Ten weeks later there may be six breeding pairs (ten pups plus the original two parents divided by two). These six breeding pairs may have a total of 60 pups. Ten for each breeding pair. We now have a total of 72 total rats or 36 breeding pairs. Ten weeks later we may have ten rats per breeding pair or 360 pups. With the 72 breeding rats we now have 432 rats. You can see how rapidly the number of rats could increase in an ideal (ideal for them, that is) environment. This is an example of exponential growth.

Linear growth would just count the number of rats bred by the original breeding pair. After three generations there would be 30 bred rats plus the two original rats or 32 rats. Allowing the pups to grow and breed results in the exponential growth. After three generations we would have 432 rats. With the rat exponential growth, as time passed the rate of increase in the numbers of rats increased dramatically. The greater the time period the greater the rate of growth of rats. I have chosen rat procreation to demonstrate the dramatic difference between linear growth and exponential growth. I also choose rat procreation to wake you up and give you a few shudders.

To reprise:

In linear growth, the rate of increase remains the same as time passes. In exponential growth, the rate of growth continually increases as time passes. The difference between exponential growth and linear growth increases dramatically over long time horizons. The longer the time horizon, the greater the difference.

The greater the percent of increase in growth per unit time period, the greater the difference. This difference is important in discussing investing. The term compounding is another term used to describe the exponential growth of an investment.

If I invest by loaning you $1000 for fifty years at ten per cent interest per year without reinvesting the interest paid, I will earn after fifty years $100 (the ten per cent interest) times fifty years equals $5000. This is linear growth of my investment.

If I invest by loaning you $1000 for fifty years at ten per cent interest per year and reinvest the interest paid each year with you at ten per cent interest, the following occurs. At the end of the first year I have earned the $100 interest. I reinvest the $100 and now have $1100 invested at ten per cent interest. The second year I earn $110 interest. I reinvest and now have $1210 invested. The third year I earn $121 in interest and have $1331 invested. After five years I have $1610.51. After ten years $2593.74. After twenty years $6,727.50. After thirty years $17,449.40. After forty years $45,259.26. After fifty years $117,390.85. This is exponential growth often called compounding.

Notice in the example described in the previous paragraph that the increase in value in the first ten years was from $1000 to $2593.74 an increase of $1593.74. This doesn't seem like much. Notice that the increase in value from year forty to year fifty was from $45,259.26 to $117,390.85 an increase of $72,131.59. Suddenly, this seems like a lot.

This example demonstrates:

**FOR EXPONENTIAL GROWTH:**

**THE IMPORTANCE AND THE EFFECT OF LENGTH OF TIME INVESTED!**

**EACH ADDITIONAL YEAR IS IMPORTANT!**

**THE IMPORTANCE OF REINVESTING THE INCOME FROM THE INITIAL INVESTMENT WHICH IS WHAT CAUSES THE EXPONENTIAL GROWTH!**

Thus $1000 invested at age twenty and kept invested for fifty years, at age seventy, will be worth significantly more than the same $1000 invested at age thirty when the investor turns seventy.

The power of compounding or exponential growth is powerful and dramatic, if and only if, the investor remains invested continually for a long period of time in an investment that increases averaged over a long enough period of time and if and only if the income from the initial investment is re-invested and not spent.

If there is anything in this chapter that you do not understand, please reread the chapter. It is important that you feel comfortable with the reasoning. It is important that you understand, somewhere deep inside you, how exponential growth works!

It is important that you understand, somewhere deep inside you:

**THE COMBINED POWER OF LONG TERM INVESTING AND EXPONENTIAL GROWTH!**

# CHAPTER THREE:
# Some Common Investing and Financial Terms

Before I delve deeper into my discussions, I need to cover the meaning of a number of financial terms. As stated earlier, if you are comfortable with all of these terms, simply skip this chapter.

What is a stock?

A stock is a part ownership of a corporation. As a part owner of the corporation, you participate in the successes and failures of the corporation. You are allowed to vote for the members of the board of directors of the corporation. You do not have additional influence over the decisions made by the managers of the corporation. Some corporations pay dividends to stock holders. Dividends are profits earned by the corporation which are paid out to the stock holders. Many corporations do not pay dividends. They prefer to use the profits each year to expand the corporation and increase the value of the corporation.

If the management makes good decisions the value of the corporation increases and the value of the stock increases. If the management does not make good decisions or external economic factors harm the corporation, the value of the stock decreases. The value of the stock varies from day to day depending on whether more investors wish to buy the stock or sell the stock. If the corporation goes bankrupt the value of the stock may disappear completely.

What is a dividend?

A dividend is a payment made by a corporation to its shareholders. Some corporations do not pay dividends. The management of some corporations prefer to keep profits and use the additional money to expand the company thereby allowing the company to increase in value. Under current tax laws dividends are taxed at the rate of ordinary income. An increase in the overall value of a company results in an increase in the price of the shares. If sold, the increased value of the stock, which you sold, is taxed as capital gains which currently are taxed at a lower rate than the income from dividends. Tax policy is continually changing.

What is a bond?

A bond is a formal loan of money by an investor to an entity such as a corporation or a country. These loans may be for short periods of time such as one year, for medium periods of time such as five or ten years and for very long periods of time such as thirty, fifty or rarely one hundred years. Fifty and one hundred-year bonds are uncommon but they exist. Bonds are bought and sold all of the time. Thus, it is possible to buy a bond which has a fractional period of time remaining, for example, seventeen and one-half years. Some bonds may be "called" by the borrower and paid off at will. This is done if the interest rate for borrowing decreases. Many bonds are fixed and may not be called.

The interest rate for a bond is fixed at a specific rate. If the current interest rates in the market drop then the value of the bond increases. If interest rates are lower investors are willing to pay more for that bond in order to obtain the cash flow (interest paid) from the bond. If the current interest rates in the market rise then the value of the bond decreases. If interest rates rise then investors will only pay less than the original value of the bond for the income stream from the bond. The longer the time period remaining in the bond, the greater the increase or decrease in the value of the bond when the interest rate changes. For long term bonds the value of the bond can change significantly with interest rate changes.

What is a mutual fund?

Many financial companies put a large collection of stocks, bonds or a mixture of stocks and bonds (Target Date Funds) into a pool and sell fractions of the value of that pool to investors. Some of these pools of assets are actively managed to try to improve investing results. Others may follow a specific index. These indexes include the DOW, which is a specific list of large company stocks, the S&P 500 which includes the 500 largest corporations and the Russell 2000 which is the smallest 2000 stocks of the largest 3000 stocks. There are a multitude of other indexes which are followed by their respective mutual funds.

The financial companies charge fees for the service of putting these collections of stock or bonds together or for managing the collection of stocks or bonds. If the investments of the mutual fund are actively managed by the financial institution, then the collection of stocks or bonds continually changes. Stocks listed in a specific index may change slowly over time.

The mutual funds which invest in bonds are often oriented toward bonds of different time periods called long term, medium term and short term bonds. They also may buy bonds from the United States government, individual cities, foreign countries, domestic corporations and foreign companies. My list of types of mutual funds is not inclusive. There are innumerable permutations and combinations of mutual funds.

When an investor buys or sells shares in a mutual fund, the actual buy/sell transaction occurs after the close of trading on the day of the transaction after the mutual fund has calculated the share value based on the values of all of the stocks or bonds at the end of trading that day.

What is an exchange traded fund or ETF?

An exchange traded fund or ETF is similar to a mutual fund in one way. The ETF is a large collection of stocks or bonds or a combination of stocks and bonds which a financial company has pooled together. The ETF may follow a specific index or it may be managed. The difference between an ETF and a mutual fund is the fact that the shares of the ETF may be bought or sold anytime the stock market is open for business. The value of the ETF shares is generally based on the actual values of the underlying stocks or bonds. Occasionally, the value of the ETF shares will deviate from exactly matching actual values of the underlying stocks or bonds

What is an annuity?

In an annuity you pay an entity, usually an insurance company, an amount of money. You may pay this money in a lump sum or a certain amount per year over a number of years. The insurance company then promises to pay you a certain amount of money per year (or per month) for the rest of your life starting on a specific agreed date.

The risk to the insurance company is that you will live much longer than average and the insurance company will lose money because it has to pay you income for longer than expected. Insurance companies do not want to lose money. They are careful and charge a lot or pay you less to keep from losing money on you.

The risks to you include you dying earlier than average and thus "wasting" the money spent buying the annuity. Another risk is that the insurance company may go bankrupt and will not exist when you are due to begin receiving payouts from your annuity. In 2008 a large insurance company would have gone bankrupt from profound financial mismanagement but was bailed out by the government. If the government had not bailed out that insurance company, the payments by the annuities of that insurance company would have decreased dramatically or ceased entirely.

A bigger risk of annuities is the risk of future inflation. The annuity contract states that you will be paid a specific amount of money per month in the future for the rest of your life. However, there will be unknown inflation in the future. The inflation will decrease the spending power of the money you receive via the annuity. The higher the inflation over the years, the less the annuity payments will be worth. If you live say 30 years and inflation is high, the annuity payments may be worth little after a few years. The loss of purchasing power of the money you receive from the annuity compounds negatively.

In essence, buying an annuity is like buying an insurance policy trying to ensure that you will have a guaranteed income from a certain specified age for the rest of your life. Think of it more as an insurance policy rather than a good investment. If you know that you are profligate and will waste your money, then buying an annuity, if you currently have the money, may be a good idea. Otherwise, it is not a good investment due to high expenses and the risk of inflation in the future.

What is inflation?

Definition:
"Inflation is a general rise in price level relative to available goods resulting in a substantial and continuing drop in purchasing power in an economy over a period of time. When the general price level rises, each unit of currency buys fewer goods and services. Consequently, inflation reflects a reduction in the purchasing power per unit of money". (Wikipedia, September 1, 2020)

While we are currently living in a prolonged period of low inflation, there is no guarantee that will last. History is replete with episodes of inflation, sometimes severe. There is no comforting or convincing reason to believe inflation will never happen again.

What is insurance?

Definition:
"Insurance is a means of protection from financial loss. It is a form of risk management, primarily used to hedge against the risk of a contingent or uncertain loss." (Wikipedia, September 1, 2020) What kinds of insurance are there? You can insure against health expenses, disability and loss of income, loss of life, accident, liability, business loss and on and on.

What is a target date fund (TDF)?

A target date fund is a mutual fund whose asset allocation becomes more conservative (higher percentage of bonds vs stocks) as the target date is approached. A target date fund usually invests in a mixture of stocks and bonds. As the fund approaches the target date, the fraction of assets that are invested in bonds increases. These funds may be managed or follow a common index like the S&P 500. Fees vary and may range from small fractions of one-percent to two percent.

I will discuss issues regarding the cost of investing later in this book. I find that the high fees many target date funds charge severely harms final investing returns. I discuss this in detail later. As you approach your target date of planned retirement, the TDF will have a much higher fraction of bonds than I think wise. I, also, discuss this later. Different TDFs allocate the fraction of stocks and bonds differently. They are not all the same.

What is a "black swan" event?

The "black swan theory" highlights the important role of rare events which have a large impact on society. These events are so unusual that computing their probability and predicting their influence is impossible. (Wikipedia, September 10, 2020; Nassim Nicholas Taleb, "The Black Swan: The Impact of the Highly Improbable, Random House, 2007)

What is diversification?

Definition:
"In finance, diversification is the process of allocating capital in a way that reduces exposure to any one particular asset or risk. A common path towards diversification is to reduce risk or volatility by investing in a variety of assets." (Wikipedia, September 10, 2020) More, much more on diversification later in this book.

What are capital gains?

If you buy a stock, a bond or other investment and later sell it for more money that you paid for it, the difference is called capital gains. If you sell the stock, bond or investment for less money than you paid for it, the difference in price is called a capital loss. At the time of this writing, the federal government and some states tax the amount of capital gains. The tax laws are complex and frequently change. I shall not attempt a discussion of today's complex tax laws which may be outdated by the time of publication. An accountant or tax lawyer can advise you. Plenty of information is available for free online. Generally, you want to decrease the amount of tax you pay to your various governments. The only time you might want to pay taxes early is if you are relatively certain that tax rates are about to rise.

# CHAPTER FOUR:
# The Psychology of Investing

Question:
Why put a chapter discussing the psychology of investing early in this book?

Answer:
How you behave, how you act, who you are will ultimately determine your success or failure in investing and in your eventual financial security or lack of same.

Definition:
"Psychology is the science of mind and behavior and includes the study of conscious and unconscious behavior as well as feelings and thoughts." (Wikipedia, September 5, 2020)

How we behave, how we save, how we invest, how we spend, the who and what we are, are determined by our mind, our behavior, our feelings, our thoughts, our conscious actions and our unconscious actions.

There is an entire field of study called behavioral economics that covers the actions of people in economic situations.

Charles Munger is a noted American investor, business man and vice chairman of Berkshire Hathaway, Inc. (Wikipedia, November 13, 2020) In a speech at Harvard in 1995 entitled "The Psychology of Human Misjudgment" he stated "How could economics not be behavioral? If it isn't behavioral, what the hell is it?"

Definition:
"Behavioral economics studies the effects of psychological, cognitive, emotional, cultural and social factors on the decisions of individuals and institutions". (Wikipedia, September 5, 2020) Nobel Prizes were awarded in 2002, 2013 and 2017 for research and advances in the intersection of psychological and economic behaviors with respect to economics and finance.

I wish to examine a few specific "patterns of behavior" that seriously impinge on our ability to navigate the tortuous waters of personal investing and personal finance. I do not propose that this chapter contains complete coverage of the complicated arena of behavioral economics. I hope that this chapter stimulates you to further self-examination and further reading.

One critical aspect of an individual's "financial behavior" is **loss aversion**.

Definition:
"Loss aversion is the tendency to prefer avoiding losses rather than obtaining an equivalent gain." (Wikipedia, September 5, 2020) Some studies suggest that the emotion attached to losses may be as much as twice as intense as the emotion attached to equivalent gains. Part of this may involve the fact that people are often deeply embarrassed by losses and don't want others to know about their losses. The emotion of regret is often stronger than the emotion of success.

Another aspect of human behavior is herd mentality or **herd behavior**.

Definition:

"Herd behavior is the behavior of individuals in a group acting collectively without central direction." (Wikipedia, September 5, 2020) Herd behavior plays a major role in the booms and busts which occur repetitively in the financial markets. When everyone seems to be buying and making money, more and more people join the herd and buy investments. Eventually there comes a point when enough people recognize the market is overpriced and a correction finally occurs.

Similarly, when the market is falling, everyone seems to be losing money and everyone seems to be selling their assets. More people join the herd and there is further selling. Eventually there comes a point when enough people realize the market is oversold and the frantic selling stops. Waves of the emotions of pessimism and optimism, namely herd behavior, often drive market prices.

There have been many attempts to analyze and predict investing herd behavior without significant success. One example is the Elliot wave principle which tried to analyze market cycles. In 1946, Ralph Nelson Elliott stated that "because man is subject to rhythmical procedure, calculations having to do with his activities can be projected far into the future with a justification and certainty heretofore unattainable." (Wikipedia, September 5, 2020)

Life, the universe and everything (tip of the hat to Douglas Adams) are too random for this kind of prediction to work. Attempts like this to predict the future ignore the rather frequent occurrences of "black swans."

Another aspect of human behavior is **escalation of commitment**.

There is a tendency to continue doing whatever you are doing even though you are losing by your actions. This is sometimes referred to as escalation of commitment. Maintaining this behavior is irrational. Yet, it is amazing how often people keep doing their losing behavior. Continuing the war in Vietnam is considered a classic example of "escalation of commitment." In responding to this behavior people often quote the common advice, "When you are digging and are deep in a hole, stop digging!" People often don't stop digging.

There have been numerous studies of decision making and investing decisions made by human beings. The short, short summary: We tend to be irrational creatures. Our decision making is often not logical.

Surveys of individual investors show repeatedly that individual investors do much worse than the stock market overall on average.

Why?

The simple reason is that individual investors tend to sell after the market (or the stock) has fallen in value, when everyone is scared. Individual investors tend to buy after the market (or the stock) has already risen in value, when everyone is excited. When the market goes up it is often a rapid rise which occurs quickly and unpredictably. If the average investor is out of the market and in cash, it is easy to miss out on the run ups.

**The average investor is NOT a long term buy and hold stock index mutual fund investor!**

It is important to know yourself, to know whether you are more impulsive or more cautious. Do you panic easily? We generally feel losses more keenly than gains. Thus, in our decision making we are often too risk averse. Years ago, a friend decided to buy shares of a specific stock for the first time. Within a few weeks the value of the stock dropped 5%. He panicked, sold and never bought another stock again. He was very risk averse. He was not thinking or investing with a long term horizon.

**How easily we are manipulated!**

When I was in college, I took a course on social psychology. We learned about a study in which people walking through an airport were asked to contribute to a legitimate charity. There were two groups in the study. In one group people were asked to donate to the charity. In the second group the people were handed a small white flower as a free gift and then asked to donate to the charity. I forget the exact numbers but something like 4% of the people who were simply asked to donate actually donated. Whereas, close to 20% of the people, handed the flower first, donated.

Why the difference? A psychological behavior called **subconscious reciprocation tendency**

If you are given a gift by someone, no matter how small the gift, you are likely to feel differently about that person and act differently. Think about it. A remarkably simple little gift changed the behavior of about one-fifth of the people asked to donate. We human beings are social animals. We learn early to respond positively to someone who gives us a gift. Sales people and others who want something from you use this social tendency to their advantage.

**How easily we are manipulated!**

When I was a practicing orthopedic surgeon drug companies often brought free lunches to my partners and the office personnel. They did this for doctors all over the country. I refused the free lunches. The drug companies were not subsidizing the restaurant industry. They were giving a free gift, the free lunch, to subtlety encourage the doctors and their office personnel to like them. Also, when you eat with someone you also feel friendlier toward them.

**How easily we are manipulated!**

Why do wealth managers give their clients free tickets and other perks? Same reason. To the wealth managers this is strictly business. They want their clients to "like" them. As you deal with financial advisors, financial managers, bankers and others who want your business, silently, mentally step back and study how they are trying to manipulate you. Believe me! They are! There is a science to it! They are not your "friend."

**How easily we are manipulated!**

Let's see how risk averse you are. If you owned any investments at the time of the 2008 crash, did you panic and sell or hold on and ride it out? If, in the future, the market dropped 5%, 10% or even 20% overnight would you panic and sell? If the market is going crazy and everyone but you seem to be making a killing, will you borrow money and buy? If your answer to these questions is "yes" then you need to be very careful how you invest your money. Long term you have a high probability of poor results.

While low cost stock index mutual funds and exchange traded funds (ETFs) seem similar, there is one huge psychological difference. I have read this statement regarding index ETFs: "Now, you can buy and sell the S&P 500 at any time!" The ETFs make buying and selling too easy, too tempting and too available. ETFs make it seductively easy to drift out of a buy and hold strategy into frequent buying and selling.

**How easily we are manipulated!**

There may be value in sticking with mutual funds for the simple psychological reason of reducing the temptation for buying when the market is "hot" and selling when the market "tanks." Many mutual funds have policies which prevent you from frequent buying and selling shares in the mutual fund. This is a good thing for both you and the fund. Choosing a low cost stock index mutual fund over an ETF to minimize the temptation to buy or sell is an example of successfully playing games with yourself. Choosing a low cost stock index mutual fund over an ETF will decrease the chances of you being manipulated into frequent buying and selling and trying to time the market.

What have others said about the psychology of investing?

In Scientific American (March 2011, Page 77) Michael Shermer, publisher of Sceptic Magazine states, "Being deeply knowledgeable on one subject narrows focus and increases confidence but also blurs the value of dissenting opinion and transforms data collection into belief conformation. One way to avoid being wrong is to be skeptical whenever you catch yourself making predictions based on reducing complex phenomena into one overarching scheme. This type of cognitive trap is why I don't make predictions and why I never will."

Quotes from Charlie Munger's Speech entitled "The Psychology of Human Misjudgment" at Harvard University in 1995:

"24 Standard Causes of Human Misjudgment." Note: I am not going to list all 24.

"My second factor is simple psychological denial."

"Third. Incentive caused bias, both in ones own mind and in ones trusted advisor, where it creates what economists call agency costs."

Definition:
"The **principal-agent problem**, in political science and economics (also known as **agency-dilemma** or the agency-problem) occurs when one person or entity (the "agent"), is able to make decisions and/or take actions on behalf of, or that impact, another person or entity: the principal. This dilemma exists in circumstances where agents are motivated to act in their own best interests which are contrary to those of their principals, and is an example of moral hazard." (Wikipedia, October 18, 2020)

"The problem arises where two parties have different interests and asymmetric information (the agent having more information), such that the principal cannot directly ensure that the agent is always acting in their (the principal's) best interest, particularly when activities that are useful to the principal are costly to the agent, and where elements of what the agent does are costly for the principal to observe (see <u>moral hazard</u> and <u>conflict of interest</u>)." (Wikipedia, October 18, 2020) (underlining in original)

I think the above two paragraphs summarize succinctly one of the most significant issues concerning the relationship between any financial advisor or financial manager and the client.

"The agency problem can be intensified when an agent acts on behalf of multiple principals (see <u>multiple principal problem</u>)." (Wikipedia, October 18, 2020) (underlining in original)

More Charlie Munger quotes:

"If you take sales presentations and brokers of commercial real estate and businesses, I'm 70 years old, I've never seen one I thought was even within hailing distance of objective truth." (Charlie Munger, 1995, Speech at Harvard University)

"Fourth, and this is a superpower in error-causing psychological tendency, bias from consistency and commitment tendency, including the tendency to avoid or promptly resolve cognitive dissonance. Includes the self-confirmation tendency of all conclusions, particularly expressed conclusions, and with a special persistence for conclusions that are hard-won." (Charlie Munger, 1995, Speech at Harvard University)

"Eight. Now this is a lollapalooza ….. bias from over-influence by social proof, that is, the conclusions of others, particularly under conditions of natural uncertainty and stress." (Charlie Munger, 1995, Speech at Harvard University)

"Bias from over-influence by authority." (Charlie Munger, 1995, Speech at Harvard University)

" …. huge insanities can come from just sub-consciously over-weighting the importance of what you are losing or almost getting and not getting." (Charlie Munger, 1995, Speech at Harvard University)

"Sam Walton won't let a purchasing agent take a handkerchief from a salesman. He knows how powerful the subconscious reciprocation tendency is. That is a profoundly correct way for Sam Walton to behave." (Charlie Munger, 1995, Speech at Harvard University)

"Munger used the term "**Lollapalooza Effect**" for multiple biases, tendencies or mental models acting in compound with each other at the same time in the same direction." … "the result is often extreme, due to the confluence of the mental models, biases or tendencies acting together, greatly increasing the likelihood of acting irrationally." … "where he explained 'three, four, five of these things work together and it turns the human brains into mush.'" (Wikipedia, November 13, 2020) (bolding original)

At the beginning of this chapter on psychology I asked a question.

Why put a chapter discussing the psychology of investing early in this book?

Let me revisit my answer.

The issue with the psychology of investing and behavioral economics is:

For successful personal financial management and investing long term, it is vital for **YOU** to understand:

**the many and various ways YOU may be manipulated**

**the many and various ways YOU may fool yourself**

**the many and various ways YOU may act against your own best interests.**

The quotes above from Michael Shermer and Charlie Munger demonstrate that this is a common and universal problem. I am not the only one concerned with these issues. You, the individual, need to be concerned with these issues. You need to learn about these issues. You need to guard against manipulation. You need to learn enough that you develop the knowledge and the self confidence to guard against these issues.

# CHAPTER FIVE:
# Who Can You Trust?

The question of "Who can you trust?" pervades much of our lives: from our love life, to the lack of reliability of the news media to financial advice. Much of what others tell us depends on their biases and motivations. Much of what others tell us is dependent on their desire to obtain something from us.

In this book I recommend against using a financial advisor or financial manager. I explain why in several places particularly in the upcoming chapters on "Cost of Investing" and "My Critique of Modern Portfolio Theory". If you do choose to use a financial advisor or financial manager, who you choose may be critical to your success or failure in investing and financial management. You need to understand your advisor's motivation and your manager's motivation. More on this later.

Let me repeat the principal-agent problem:

Definition:
"The principal-agent problem, in political science and economics (also known as agency-dilemma or the agency-problem) occurs when one person or entity (the "agent"), is able to make decisions and/or take actions on behalf of, or that impact, another person or entity: the principal. This dilemma exists in

circumstances where agents are motivated to act in their own best interests which are contrary to those of their principals, and is an example of moral hazard." (Wikipedia, October 18, 2020)

**NEVER TRUST ANY ONE PERSON WITH YOUR MONEY!**

The big financial firms as a place to keep your assets, yes. Preferably, a non-profit financial firm. An individual or small, one-person firm, NO! The successful con men and con women (for parity's sake) often start taking in money from friends, members of their church group or other social group. If the con person is a member of your social group you are much more likely, to trust that person. DON'T!

Here are a few of my personal stories.

First:
In the mid 1950s as a young boy, I watched my father invest in stock in the Brunswick-Balke Corporation, which was selling a new bowling pinsetter machine. Brunswick-Balke, in the mid 1950s, was touted as one of the best stocks to invest in. The stock rocketed up and I observed my father's excitement as the value of the stock soared. Then in the early 1960s, the bowling market became saturated and the value of the Brunswick-Balke stock plummeted. I also watched my father's disappointment as the value of the stock fell sharply.

In my limited experience as a child, I developed a deep abiding fear of the volatility, the uncertainty, the risk of the value of any single stock. I also watched how the advice of my father's financial advisor failed to meet expectations.

Second:
At one point, in the first year of our marriage my wife and I had a net worth of $50. All of it deposited in our bank checking account. True! In the mid

1980s, my wife and I finally saved enough money to consider investing it in "something." We lacked any experience in investing. I had done some limited reading about investing.

So, with a few thousand dollars to invest I made an appointment with a stock broker (shall I call him an investment advisor, financial manager or financial advisor?) at one of the well-known, supposedly reputable financial companies. I picked the company because of its sterling reputation. The name of the company is not really important. If I don't mention the name, I avoid risk of lawsuit for deserved defamation of character. The stock broker recommended a mutual fund. He showed me a graph of a continuous upward trend in the value of shares in this mutual fund.

This mutual fund had, as I recall, a "load" of 6 ½%. It may have been 6 ¾%. This happened many years ago so that detail is uncertain. This "load" was what is called a "front end sales charge." Let's say I am investing $10,000. The load or front-end sales charge is 6 ½% of $10,000 or 0.065 X $10,000 equals $650. The broker and his financial company are paid $650 immediately. Not a bad hourly wage given my half-hour meeting with the stock broker. Meanwhile, my investment starts out worth only $9350, not the $10,000, I started with. My investment then has to increase by 6.95% in order for me to simply break even. The reason I have to earn a greater per cent to break even (compared with the per cent load) is that I am starting with less money invested after paying the front-end sales charge.

Back to my meeting with the stock broker. By this point, I had done enough reading to have read the advice "never" to pay a large load for a mutual fund. Having done this reading prior to the meeting, I laughed at the 6 ½ % load, congratulated the stock broker on his cleverness at finding a mutual fund with such a large load and walked out. I have never dealt with that financial company since.

**Who can you trust?**

In this investment advisor vs. client interaction, the investment advisor was acting in his personal short term interest to obtain the largest fee he could as quickly as he could. He was not acting in my (the investor's) interest. Had he been acting in his long-term interest, he might have made a different recommendation. I might have stayed with him. He might have earned more on commissions earned over the years. However, he was focused on his short term interest. My (the investor's interest) did not matter.

This is a clear example of the moral hazard of the principal-agent problem discussed above.

I have previously mentioned the concept of the "time horizon" for investing in the chapter on exponential growth. I discuss this in even more detail in the chapter on cost of investing. For the moment, understand that you, the investor, should have a time horizon of ten or more years. Hopefully, you are young enough to consider that your investment time horizon is as long as forty or fifty years. The investment advisor has a time horizon for you of a day or at most a month. If the value of your portfolio drops too much in any one day or any one month, you may pull out your money and switch advisors.

**There exists a significant difference in the investment time horizon of your financial advisor or financial manager and your own personal investment time horizon.**

More, much more on this later. The different investing time horizons of the financial manager and the client/investor results in the clear and present danger of encountering the principal-agent problem.

**Who can you trust?**

Third:
Another of my personal stories regarding who can you trust. Many years ago, my group's profit-sharing plan was being managed by a financial firm

with offices in Boston. I flew up to Boston one time to visit our investment advisor/manager in his office. During the course of our meeting, I asked our financial advisor/manager this question.

"You are managing a number of different profit-sharing plans, all of which have the same long term goals and the same long term time horizons. Do you manage the investments for all of the firms the same way? Do you buy the same stocks and bonds for each account or do you manage them differently? If you manage them differently, how and why?"

Before you read further, before you move on to the next page,

**STOP!**

and think about this question.

Should this investment advisor/manager buy the exact same stocks and/or bonds for all of the accounts under management that have the same long term investing horizon and same long term goals?

What answer do you expect?

Why do you expect that answer?

What answer should be the "right" answer?

Why should that be the "right" answer?

Please think about this for a while before moving on to the next page!

Welcome back!

Our financial manager's answer: He bought different stocks and different bonds for each profit-sharing plan account. His reasoning? Just like you, as an individual, should diversify your investments, so that one bad investment does not ruin your overall results, **he diversified his advice (management) so that one bad group of investments would not ruin his overall investment management results**. Thus, he was not risking having all of his clients leave him at the same time as the result of bad luck in his choice of investments for the accounts.

Does his answer surprise you?

It sure surprised me! In retrospect, perhaps, I was not that surprised. Otherwise, why would I have asked him that question?

Do you realize that financial managers are diversifying their advice? Do you realize you are not necessarily getting their best advice?

If you are using a financial manager, is this information causing you to question what you are doing? If you are using a financial manager, is this information causing you to question what your financial manager is doing?

It should!

Prior to my meeting with our investment advisor/manager, I had already decided that our group was going to stop using this manager. I appreciated his honesty. I must confess that I was surprised by his honesty. I truly respect him for his honesty. But really! Think about it. We were not being given his "best" advice and management. I suspect many investment advisors and managers do the same.

The fact that this financial manager was diversifying his management decisions "to protect himself" is another example of the moral hazard of the principal-agent problem. The principal-agent problem is pervasive. It's everywhere! It's everywhere! It's everywhere!

**Who can you trust?**

I had already decided that we were going to move from managed investing to almost all stocks in low cost United States stock index funds. The cost of investing is important. More, much more about the cost of investing later.

Fourth:
This next personal story is an embarrassing one. There is a common saying that if something sounds too good to be true, it probably is. I had heard this. I knew this. Yet, in my early learning phase I fell into this trap all by myself. Not really all by myself. Friends of mine helped me along the road. My friends were investing in the drilling of an oil well in Texas and encouraged me to join. So, I did. The organizer of this investment guaranteed to refund our money if the oil well came in dry. Silly, silly us. More to the point: Silly, silly me! We believed him. One of my friends even travelled to Texas to inspect the oil well to ensure that the investment was valid. The well came in dry. Our money was not refunded. We lost 100% of our investment. The promise of refund was, of course, a total scam. I fell for it as did my friends.

In my writing, if I seem a wee tad skeptical, a wee tad paranoid, a wee tad distrustful, a wee tad wary, if I keep asking,

**"Who can you trust?"**

Believe me, I earned my spurs.

Fifth:
Most of you are probably familiar with the Bernie Madoff con story. His cleverness lay in refusing some people's money. Thus, he set up the psychology for others to strive to be part of the "IN" crowd and get their money accepted for investment.

**How we are manipulated!**

This brings me to a NEVER.

**NEVER invest your money with an individual.**

NEVER! NEVER! NEVER.

Let me repeat.

NEVER! NEVER! NEVER!

The safety and the security of your money is only as good as the trustworthiness of the individual taking your money. As Bernie Madoff demonstrated "convincingly", good scam artists are amazingly convincing.

**Who can you trust?**

Sixth:

Another "Who can you trust?" story. A few years ago, the country of Libya, using the Libya Investment Authority invested approximately one billion dollars ($1,000,000,000) under the direction of a well-known and well-respected international financial firm. All or most of the money was invested in complex, hard to understand, "risky" investments. Within a short period of time this massive investment lost 95% of its value.

**"Who can you trust?"**

The Libya Investment Authority sued the financial firm. The financial firm won the lawsuit. The financial firm did not lose money. In fact, the financial firm benefited greatly from the fees they charged. Clearly, the advice and management of the Libyan funds was seriously deficient.

This is yet another example of the moral hazard of the principal-agent problem. The principal-agent problem is pervasive. It's everywhere. It's everywhere. It's everywhere.

One of many problems with the Libya Investment Authority complex investments was the investment's lack of transparency.

**Lack of transparency** is a problem with many investments peddled in the financial marketplace. More on this later.

Here is a question which fascinates me: This story about the Libyan Investment Authority loss is common knowledge. The story was highlighted in newspapers. Here is a question whose answer I simply do not understand. Why does anybody continue to deal with that investment firm?

I repeat:

Why does anybody continue to deal with that investment firm? I mean, seriously, why would anyone trust this financial firm again. Yet this firm continues to be busy and successful.

There is a large bank in which multiple employees were opening fraudulent additional accounts for account holders. This story, too, is well-known and was highlighted in newspapers. Yet the bank is still in business and doing well. Why would anyone trust that bank again? Yet people do.

Why do so many people continue to trust institutions which have clearly and publicly failed in their fiduciary capacity to look out for the best interests of their customers?

Why do so many people continue to trust institutions which have clearly and publicly succumbed to the moral hazard of the principal-agent problem?

**Who can you trust?**

Seventh:

As I am writing this, I notice an announcement in the newspapers on September 23, 2020 which states that a major international financial firm is nearing an agreement with federal prosecutors and regulators to pay a fine to settle civil and criminal charges that its traders rigged futures and securities markets.

Once again, a major financial firm is caught rigging the system. Once again, a major international financial firm has failed in its fiduciary responsibility to its clients. Once again, a major international financial firm has succumbed to the moral hazard of the principal-agent issue.

**Who can you trust?**

Find out who these firms are. Then NEVER and I mean NEVER deal with them.

**"Who can you trust?"**

Sadly, very few!!!

Eighth:

I have a policy, that you may only lie to me once. If I catch you in a lie, thereafter, I know that I cannot trust you. Regardless of whether you apologize to me or not. Regardless of whether I accept the apology or not. I know that I cannot trust you as I did before. If you read about the improper behavior of any company, and I mean any company, why ever deal with them again?

**"Who can you trust?"**

Ninth:

The same policy (you may only lie to me once), I suppose, should also apply to politicians and the media. Lie to me once and I should never trust you again. Lie to me twice and why would I ever trust you again. With respect to politicians, unfortunately that means you will never believe any of them, anytime, anywhere. And the media? This book is not about the media, but I have two suggestions.

First:
Watch some congressional hearing or candidate debate so that you, yourself, observe precisely what happens and hear precisely what is said. Decide for yourself exactly what you heard and what you saw.

Then immediately go online and survey many news websites: for example, in alphabetical order: ABC News, AP News, CBS News, CNN News, Fox News, MSNBC News, NBC News, New York Times, Reuters, Wall Street Journal, Washington Post. Pick other websites if you wish.

Following your own personal survey of the news websites, ask yourself: Which news organizations were closer to the truth? Which websites exhibited bias in what they covered? Which websites exhibited bias in what they did not cover? Which websites exhibited bias in how they covered it?

Second:
For some news worthy event or occurrence, do the same survey of all of these websites. Add others if you choose. Again, ask yourself the same questions:

Which news organizations are closer to the truth? Which news organizations exhibit bias in what they choose to cover? Which news organizations exhibit bias in what they chose not to cover? Which news organizations exhibit bias in how they cover the event? If you find news organizations which exhibit clear bias in their coverage, why ever watch them again?

The question of: "Who can you trust?" is becoming more and more urgent in the midst of our world of political and economic uncertainty! The question of: "Who can you trust?" is vital in your financial dealings!

What have others said?

Per Wikipedia (October 8, 2020) Burton Malkiel is an American economist, author of the book, "A Random Walk Down Wall Street", professor of economics at Princeton and was a director at Vanguard Group for 28 years.

In the Wall Street Journal (May 29, 2013, Page A15) Burton G. Malkiel starts out stating, "From 1980 to 2006, the U.S. financial services sector grew from 4.9% to 8.3% of GDP. A substantial share of that increase represented **increases in asset-management fees**." He later states, "In my judgement, **investors have received no benefit from this increase in expense ratios**." He continues later, "The increase in fees could be justified if it reflected increasing returns for investors from active management, or if it improved the efficiency of the market. Neither of these arguments holds. **Actively managed funds of publicly traded securities have consistently underperformed index funds-by roughly the differential in fees charged**." (bolding mine) (GDP is gross domestic product, which is the total value of goods and services produced in a country each year)

He continues in the next paragraph, "**Passive portfolios that held all the stocks in a broad-based market index have substantially outperformed the average active manager since 1980.** Therefore, the increase in fees likely represents a deadweight loss for investors." Malkiel later asks, "Why do investors continue to pay such high fees for financial services of such questionable value? Many may incorrectly judge the quality of investment advice by the price charged." (bolding mine)

In the Washington Post (January 27, 2013) in his column, Barry Ritholtz emphasizes, "**Fear, higher volatility and significant drawdowns derail all but the most disciplined investors**. As soon as trouble shows up, they are gone." He also adds, "Steer clear of venture capital and private equity …. What is available to you are the leftovers-typically what the VCs have already picked over and passed on." He also states, "**Avoid new financial products at all costs. New financial products are seemingly created all the time. They tend to be complex, expensive and dangerous**. For the most part, they are designed primarily to capture a fee for the underwriters." (bolding mine) (VC means venture capital)

**"Who can you trust?"**

## CHAPTER SIX:
# Risk Revisited; Inflation Revisited; Safety Revisited

Congratulations! For the first time in your life you have some money to invest. What to do? What is the "best" investment? Do you want a "safe" investment? What is a "safe" investment? Is there a "safe" investment?

Simple Question:

**What is safe?**

Is "safe" really and truly "safe?"

Simple Answer:

**Nothing, repeat nothing, repeat nothing is truly "safe."**

I repeat:

Nothing is really and truly safe. Nothing. Now if that isn't a scary statement, I don't know what is.

If by "safe" you mean absolutely, positively no chance of losing any of your money then "safe" does not exist.

I repeat:

Absolute safety with respect to money does not exist. Period. End of discussion.

I repeat:

**Absolute safety with respect to money does not exist.**

If you had $10,000 in $100-dollar bills stashed in a safety deposit box in a bank at the World Trade Center, that money was incinerated and lost in the airplane terror attack of 9/11. In exceptional circumstances, even a safety deposit box is not "safe."

How about keeping your money in your mattress? Your house can burn down. Some years ago, I read of a woman in Israel who kept a large sum of money in her mattress and did not tell her family. One day her family threw out the old mattress and bought her a new mattress as a surprise. All of her money was lost! Even the mattress may not be safe.

Let's ignore the risk of catastrophic loss of the money in the safety deposit box or mattress for a moment.

Inflation has been a continuing process for a long time.

What is inflation?

Definition:
"Inflation may be defined as a general increase in prices and/or a corresponding decrease in the purchasing value of money over time." (Wikipedia, September 17, 2020)

This means that over time the number price of items for sale increases. It also means that the amount of something that you can buy for $100 decreases over time. Deflation, which is the reverse, only occurs during times of severe economic downturns. Recently, inflation in the United States has been relatively low, around 2% per year. In 1778 inflation was approximately 30% per year. In 1917 inflation was approximately 20% per year. In 1980 inflation was approximately 13.5% per year. Between 1965 and 1982 the United States experienced sufficient year in year out inflation that those years are now called by some the years of the "Great Inflation." (www.federalreservehistory.org, August 20, 2020)

The budget deficit in the United States has recently ballooned, seemingly out of control.

There may exist an underlying flaw in modern democracies, in which politicians will forever promise and pay for more than they are able or willing to tax for. The pathetic inability of politicians to resist overspending may well be our eventual ruin.

For the moment the United States is seen internationally as the bastion of safety and stability. I think that is the reason that the United States government continues to be able to borrow money at staggeringly low interest rates. This may change at any time. This may change suddenly at any time. The probability that inflation will return sometime in the future seems to me near certainty.

There is a rule of 72. This is a quick way to estimate the effect of inflation on the value of money. Divide the inflation rate into 72. The answer estimates the number of years it takes for the value of your money to drop by half. Thus, for an inflation rate of 10%, divide 10 into 72. The value of money halves in a little over seven years. Given the inflation rate of 13.5% in 1980, if that rate continued the value of money would halve in only 5 1/3 years. That is a horrifying and rapid drop in the value of any cash you are holding! High inflation is brutal! If you held cash in a safety deposit box during those years, the value of your money, the number of "things" you could buy for your money halved in about 5 1/3 years. Now, that is scary.

**Conclusion: Holding on to cash is not safe! Holding on to cash guarantees a continuing loss equal to the rate of inflation.**

With inflation above 10%, how could you ever save enough for retirement? I remember the late 1970s and early 1980s. One of the major concerns, of the people I knew, was the fact that you could never save and invest enough to be comfortable in retirement. Inflation would rapidly destroy the value of your retirement savings. The rule of 72 calculation discussed above demonstrates that keeping your money in a bank account, money market fund or safety deposit box is "not safe." Keeping your assets in cash during times of high inflation is a sure way to lose value quickly.

This advice does not pertain to any money you plan to use in the next five to seven years. Any money you plan to use in the next five to seven years should be kept in cash or cash-like instruments like certificates of deposit or money market funds. For example, money you are saving for a down payment on a house should be kept in cash or cash-like instruments.

I repeat:

If you hide cash somewhere, you are guaranteeing a continual and persistent loss of value over time. The higher the inflation rate, the faster the hidden money loses value. .

There is risk in everything we do, including investing.

There is, however, a marked difference in the "risk of investing" depending on whether you are a long term buy and hold investor or you do frequent buying and selling.

Over the past one hundred years the stock market has "on average" gone up significantly over most ten-year periods and over all time periods of twenty years or longer. Of course, we all know the saying, "Past experience is no guarantee of future performance."

**A LONG TERM BUY AND HOLD STRATEGY WITH LOW COST UNITED STATES STOCK INDEX FUNDS WILL OUTPERFORM ANY OTHER STRATEGY FOR MOST OF US REAL, AVERAGE, PASSIVE INVESTORS.**

In the rest of this book, I discuss many other issues and strategies for minimizing long term investing risk and for maximizing the probability of good long term investing returns.

**THIS ENTIRE BOOK IS ORIENTED TOWARD MINIMIZING LONG TERM INVESTING RISK.**

**THIS ENTIRE BOOK IS ORIENTED TOWARD MAXIMIZING THE PROBABILITY OF GOOD LONG TERM INVESTING RETURNS.**

Let me emphasize:

Short term investing is gambling pure and simple. I offer no information for doing this successfully. Many who try this will either lose money or suffer sub-optimal investing results.

**Long term investing with moderate diversification, emphasis on stocks and using low cost United States stock index mutual funds has, based on the past one hundred years of investing history, the best chance for obtaining best investing results for you, the "ordinary, passive investor".**

In the following chapters on "Cost of Investing" and "My Critique of Modern Portfolio Theory" I address the difference between short term investing risk and long term investing risk. Modern Portfolio Theory and most financial advisors and financial managers are fixated on short term investing risk rather than long term investing risk. More, much more about investing risk in those chapters.

If this chapter on risk seems incomplete, understand that this entire book deals with the question of minimizing your "risk" of poor long term investment returns and maximizing your chances of "best" long term investment returns.

More, much more about risk and investing to come.

# CHAPTER SEVEN:
# The Cost of Investing

Earlier, I mentioned my first experience with a stock broker who recommended a mutual fund with a 6 ½% load. That vignette, that early experience, demonstrated to me the importance of evaluating the cost of investing. The issue of the cost of investing gets a separate chapter of its own. This is one of the most important chapters in this book.

**MINIMIZING THE YEARLY COST OF YOUR INVESTING IS CRITICAL TO YOUR LONG TERM INVESTING RESULTS.**

**BY CRITICAL, I MEAN, CRITICAL!**

Let's look at a yearly investment cost of 1%.

If you invest $1000 at ten per cent per year compounding for forty years you will have $45,259.26 ignoring taxes. That is, you will have slightly more than 45 times your initial investment. Recall my discussion of the effect of compounding with long time horizons. If your cost of investing is 1% per year, you, in effect, are investing $1000 at nine per cent per year. After forty years you will have earned $31,409.42. This difference is a huge.

Stop and reread the last paragraph.

That one per cent cost per year is not trivial. That one percent per year cost is compounded negatively over forty years. That 1% cost per year decreased the final investing result to only 69% of what it would have been without the 1% yearly cost.

If you invest $1000 at ten per cent per year compounding for fifty years you will have $117,390.85 ignoring taxes. Again, notice the different result from the extra ten years of investing. $117,390.85 versus $45,259.26.

If you allow for a 1% per year investing cost over that fifty-year period, thus investing at 9% per year, you would have $74,357.52 after fifty years. The difference is $117,390.85 versus $74,357.52.

Notice again, the extra ten years of investment shows an increasing difference in final investing result that the 1% per year cost causes. At fifty years, the difference in your investment result was 63% of what it might have been.

The longer the time interval the greater the percentage difference caused by the yearly cost of investing.

Let's look at a yearly investment cost of 2%.

If you invest $1000 at ten per cent per year compounding for fifty years you will have $117,390.85 ignoring taxes as noted above. With a 2% per year cost, you are, in essence, investing at 8% per year. If you invest $1000 at eight per cent per year compounding for fifty years you will have $46,901.61 ignoring taxes. The final investment result after fifty years is 40% of what it otherwise would have been. Compare $117,390.85 versus $46,901.6.

Look at the difference a 2% yearly cost of investing made over 50 years!

(This is pure human interest: Calculations made using my retro Hewlett-Packard HP12C handheld financial calculator; a workhorse still going strong; this calculator was written up in the Wall Street Journal, May 4, 2011, headline of article: Wall Street's Cult Calculator Turns 30)

I repeat:

With a fifty-year investment time horizon, a 2% per year investment cost will lead to a final investment result approximately 40% of what it might have been, everything else being equal.

Consider this:

If you are thinking of investing and leaving an inheritance for your children and grandchildren, you have an investing horizon of greater than fifty years.

Large pension funds, university endowments, inter-generational trust funds and any other investment entities with a 50 year or greater time horizon, take note!

The cost of investment is critical to your long term horizon investing results.

The same is true for any ordinary, average, passive investor.

**THE PERCENTAGE DIFFERENCES ARE THE SAME REGARDLESS OF HOW MUCH MONEY IS INVESTED!**

The calculated percentage differences are the same if you invest $100 or $50,000,000,000. More about pension funds and their investing results ahead.

I repeat:

The amount of money invested does not change the math with respect to the percentage change caused by the cost of investing.

So, how do you, an ordinary, passive investor "control" your investment costs.

**DITCH ANY FINANCIAL ADVISOR OR FINANCIAL MANAGER WHO CHARGES YOU A PERCENTAGE OF YOUR TOTAL INVESTED ASSETS EVERY YEAR!**

How is that for being heretical?

I repeat:

**DITCH ANY FINANCIAL ADVISOR OR FINANCIAL MANAGER WHO CHARGES YOU A PERCENTAGE OF YOUR TOTAL INVESTED ASSETS EVERY YEAR!**

Seek advice, if you wish, from tax accountants, estate lawyers or financial advisors who charge by the hour.

Statistics show that most actively managed funds which charge a yearly percentage of total assets invested underperform the index funds for any ten-year period studied.

There, is no way to predict ahead of time which managed funds will be the few that outperform for that ten-year period.

It is strange. It seems counter intuitive. It does not seem to make common sense. That two percent cost per year seems so little.

Yet, the influence of compounding, i.e. the influence on the exponential growth of your investment portfolio, over a fifty year time horizon is staggering.

A two percent per year "cost of investing" will decrease your final investment result, given a fifty-year time horizon, to approximately 40% of what it might have been.

Your financial advisors and financial managers, who charge you high fees, will conveniently forget to explain this to you.

You have to think for yourself and not just rely on your financial advisors and financial managers.

I repeat:

You have to think for yourself and not just rely on your financial advisors and financial managers.

**AM I EXAGGERATING?**

How might your investment cost reach 2% per year? Look up the "cost of investing", that is the "fees" for a number of RIAs, which are "Registered Investment Advisors."

Definition:
"A registered investment adviser (RIA) is a firm that is an investment adviser in the United States, registered as such with the Securities and Exchange Commission or a state's securities agency." (Wikipedia, September 24, 2020)

More from Wikipedia. "Registered investment adviser firms receive compensation in the form of fees for providing financial advice and investment management. They are required to act as a fiduciary. This is very different from broker-dealers and their representatives, who provide recommendations for a commission. **Broker dealers and their representatives are not required to act as a fiduciary**. This is a different standard of care, but most consumers are unaware of the difference, as **any of these professionals may call themselves a financial advisor.**" (Wikipedia, September 24, 2020) (bolding mine)

Let me repeat the definition of a "fiduciary."

"A fiduciary is a person who holds a legal or ethical relationship of trust with one or more other parties (person or group of persons). Typically, a fiduciary takes care of money or assets for another person." (Wikipedia, August 21, 2020)

More on:

**AM I EXAGGERATING?**

How might your investment cost reach 2% per year? If your financial advisor or financial manager charges you 1% of your invested value per year for the advice and management and then invests your assets in mutual funds which charge 1% per year, you can reach an investment cost of 2% per year quite easily.

Many Registered Investment Advisors have yearly fees which reach 1.5% per year sometimes more. They may also charge additional fees for the cost of trades, etc. Many years ago, when I was still in my "learning" phase, I briefly invested in a hedge fund which charged 2% per year. After three years the hedge fund underperformed the market by 2% per year. I withdrew my money. As I said before, "I have earned my spurs."

These registered investment advisors will not inform you, counsel you, educate you or instruct you that their yearly fees compounded over thirty, forty or fifty years will seriously impact your final investment results.

These so called "fiduciaries" earn a lot of money by "managing your money." They are not in the business of educating you into "full" financial independence. Of course not. They would be putting themselves out of business.

Personal story:
I have a friend whose mother left some money in a trust fund for her grandchildren. The bank's trust fund department managing the trust fund was charging 1 ¼% of the total assets per year to manage this trust. This friend

occasionally asked me for financial advice. At one point the trust department of this well known, internationally respected bank was placing the stock investment assets in this trust into an actively managed mutual fund which was charging 2% of total assets per year.

What was the total yearly investment cost for the stock investments in this trust fund? A staggering 3 ¼% per cent per year. I am not making this up!

When my friend asked the trust manager to transfer the money to a low-cost stock index mutual fund, he flat out refused. Personally, I suspect the trust official was getting financial kickbacks for investing in that mutual fund. Otherwise, I have little explanation for his behavior.

I repeat:

The combination of the trust manager's fees and the 2% mutual fund fees raised the "cost of investing" for stocks in this trust to 3 ¼ % per year.

I have personal experience with watching a trust fund's financial manager make decisions which resulted in a per year cost of greater than 3 %. Recall, this was in a trust fund for children. This was in a trust fund with a long term investing horizon of the children's lifetime. This was in a trust fund with a long term investing horizon of perhaps seventy or eighty years. Think of the compounding effect of a year in and year out investing cost of more than 3 % per year over seventy to eighty years.

I am going to whip out my HP12C calculator. Let's examine investing $1000 as in the example I used above. Investing $1000 at 10% and compounding for let's say 60 years results in an investing result of $304,481.64. Now, allow for a yearly investing cost of 3 ¼ %. Thus, we are investing $1000 at 6.75% for 60 years. The final result is $50,358.53. The final result given the greater cost of investing and the longer time horizon leads to a final investing result which is less than 1/6 th of what it might have been! Note how the increased length of time invested and the greater yearly cost of investing led to this staggering difference. Had this horrific mismanagement been allowed to continue, the eventual cost to the grandchildren would have been huge. One final thought. The grandchildren would never know how their "trust" had been abused.

The 3 ¼ % cost of investing mentioned above happened to my friend's trust fund. This was real! Fortunately my friend's mother's instructions regarding the management of the trust fund allowed for the transfer of assets to another trust company or bank at will. With that threat, the trust fund manager relented and transferred the assets to a low-cost stock mutual fund.

As I stated before, I have earned my spurs. I have witnessed examples of profoundly bad financial management and advice.

There is another lesson here.

**If you write up trust fund documents for a trust for your family, allow for the transfer of assets to another reputable trust company or trust department of a large financial firm.**

This is insurance against what I saw happen, namely investment management which was deliberately, fraudulently and/or ineptly bad.

More on the cost of investing. Let's look at the cost of investing from another perspective. My memory is that I read this in one of Warren Buffet's letters to shareholders in one of the annual reports of The Berkshire Hathaway. I have tried to find which one and failed to find it. What I have to say may not be exactly what Warren Buffet said.

Think of this. Take all of the companies in the world in a given year who have shareholders who own stock in those companies. All of these companies in the world make a certain profit in aggregate that year. Some of the profits are paid to the world's shareholders as dividends and the rest of the profits kept within the companies result in increased value of the world's companies.

Do the profits of all of the shareholder companies of the world accrue to the all of the "shareholders of the world?"

They should, shouldn't they?

But, they don't.

Why?

Let's factor in the yearly cost of investing, Let's assume your personal cost of investing is 1% per year. Let's expand to assume, for this example, that all of the shareholders of the world have a cost of investing of 1% per year.

This means that 1% of the total value of all the companies in the world is being transferred to the financial managers and financial advisors of the world each year! Not, 1% of the profits of these companies, but 1% of the total value of all of the companies of the world! Recall that every buy and sell is, in essence, a zero sum game. The buying and the selling do not change the value of the profits of all of the shareholder companies of the world.

Please stop and reread the above paragraph again.

Let me repeat:

If the average yearly cost of investing for all of the world's shareholders is 1% per year, this means that 1% of the total value of all the companies in the world is being transferred to the financial managers and financial advisors of the world each year. Not, 1% of the profits of these companies, but 1% of the total value of all of the companies of the world.

Following this reasoning, roughly 10% of the value of all of the shareholder companies in the world would be transferred to the financial advisors and financial managers of the world over each decade, ignoring for the moment the issue of compounding.

Over a long period of time this amounts to a massive transfer of wealth from the owners of the companies, that is, the shareholders of the companies to the financial managers and financial advisors of the shareholders of the world.

I just used 1% as an example. As stated above it is easy for your cost of investment to be greater that 1% per year. Obviously, there are investors with lower investment costs per year.

Is your financial manager or financial advisor really worth that much?

Remember, for each buy and each sell there is a counter party taking the exact opposite position. Ignoring the minor cost of the transaction, each buy and sell is a zero sum game. The whole situation though is not a zero sum game.

The winners of this seemingly zero sum "game" are the financial managers and financial advisors.

They continue to earn their fees regardless of which side of each buy and sell transaction they are on.

In my own lexicon, your personal "yearly cost of investing' is what I call a "known risk" of investing. Black swan events, in my lexicon, are more or less "unknown risks."

Your personal cost of investing in a "known risk" which you are able to control.

How?

Examine your investments carefully. What is your yearly cost of investing? Is your investment manager or financial advisor worth your yearly cost? Probably not!

**A high "yearly cost of investing" is a "known risk" which you can eliminate.**

What about 401K plans?

What about the "yearly investment cost" of 401k plans. For many years, on my advice, my group of orthopedic surgeons placed about 95% of our profit sharing assets and 401K plan assets in low cost United States stock index institutional mutual funds at a major financial firm. Our yearly investment cost was about 0.16 % per year. All of the funds were pooled. Each year we paid an accounting firm to account for the year end summary of assets for each participant. The accounting firm's fees amounted to a miniscule percentage of the total assets invested. Thus, in our corporate profit-sharing plan and 401K investments our yearly investing cost was less than 0.2% per year. Fees in many institutions have decreased since then.

At one point our orthopedic group joined a large group of orthopedic surgeons and the investment plan of the larger group was run by one of the large financial firms. The basic yearly cost for each participant in the plan run by the large financial firm was about 0.75%. Then there was an additional fee for each specific fund you chose to invest in. This ran the yearly fee (the yearly cost of investing) easily over 1% per year unless you chose the lowest cost index fund. In that case your yearly cost of investing was just under 1% per year. You couldn't avoid the high yearly cost of investing.

CEOs of corporations take note!

I believe most corporate plans have expenses which are too high and harm your personal investing results and the investing results of all of your employees. Surely, there are less expensive ways to run your corporation's profit sharing plans and 401k plans. It should be possible for corporations to join together, offer a limited number of ultra low cost institutional index funds, combine the accounts, hire your own accountants to keep track of the individual accounts and drastically lower your yearly cost of investing for you and all of your employees. At least, you could offer that as an option to your employees.

Back to our corporate 401k plan:

Our corporate plan allowed for the transfer of funds to a roll-over IRA after age fifty. I took advantage of that as soon as we switched to the corporate plan.

If you are invested in one of these expensive corporate 401K type plans, transfer your money to an individual roll-over IRA as soon as you reach the age at which you are allowed to do so.

Make sure the 401k assets are transferred from your retirement account directly to another retirement account to avoid a taxable event.

The financial firms are earning big bucks on these corporate plans.

What about 529 plans?

529 plans allow for the tax-free investing of money for a child's or grandchild's education. Details you can look up online. I examined a number of these plans and found the fees unreasonably high! Investigate the fees! Recently, some of the financial firms have lowered their fees. Thus, if you invest money in a 529 plan, investigate the fees, pick the financial firm with the lowest fee and invest only in the lowest cost United States stock index mutual fund offered.

The following example is for the financial managers of public pension funds and university endowments. Presidents of universities and members of the university boards of directors take note! Members of state legislatures take note!

The investing time horizon of the financial managers of public pension funds and university endowments should be 100 years or more. Why? They expect to remain in existence for centuries.

Consider this quote: "...large endowments pay on average a steep 1.6% annual fee -- exactly the amount by which they underperform the middle-class investors 401(k) index fund." (Marketwatch website, October 25, 2020, article by Michael Edesses) Note that the quote stated that a 1.6% annual fee was the "average." That suggests that roughly half of the endowments have higher yearly expenses. In a following chapter, "My Critique of Modern Portfolio Theory", I examine the investing results of CalPERS, the $400 billion dollar pension fund of California.

Whip out my HP 12C hand held calculator. $1000 invested at 10% per year for 100 years, reinvesting the interest, reaches a value of $13,780,612. Subtract the 1.6% fees which the universities are paying on average. Then, $1000 invested at 8.4% per year for 100 years, reinvesting the interest, reaches a value of $3,183,671. The negative effect of the 1.6% fee compounded over 100 years results in a final investment performance of 23% of what it would have been without the 1.6% fee. That 1.6% per year cost, compounded over one hundred years, resulted in a final investing result less than one fourth of what it could have been and should have been. Astounding!

Large university endowments and public pension funds could really get their costs down. Large endowments and public pension funds could easily improve their long term investment results. They don't. More on this later.

You, an average passive investor, can beat the large endowments and the public pension funds simply by keeping your investing costs down!

How?

Read and reread this book!

I am not the only one discussing these issues. Hopefully, I will be the one you listen to!

I repeat: The performance of the low cost United States stock index mutual funds is NOT, repeat NOT dependent on the amount of money invested. The percentage results are the same for any amount invested.

Here is the crux of the matter.

Each time the stock market crashes, people say "This time is different!"

Will you be able to resist panic selling in each and every horrific downturn?

If you answer is "Yes" you will do well long term.

If your answer is "No" and/or your investing behavior results in "panic selling," then you will not do well investing long term.

I can only advise against panic selling during a major downturn and hope you are able to resist panic selling when "blood is in the streets" and the "smell of fear" is pervasive.

Reprise:

For investment advice, I think this chapter on the "yearly cost of investment" may be the most important one in this book.

**Aggressively, keeping your "yearly cost of investment" low will have a profound, positive influence on your investment results forty to fifty years in the future. Keeping your "yearly cost of investment" low involves ditching expensive financial advisors, financial managers, Registered Investment Advisors, hedge funds or other financial entities which charge a percentage of your total invested assets each year.**

What have others said?

From the Wall Street Journal (March 23, 2012, Page A15) Burton Malkiel writes, "**In today's environment, the minimization of investment fees is more important than ever.** A 1% investment management fee may appear to be very low when measured against assets. But when measured against a 7% equity return, that fee represents more than 14% of the return. Against a 2% dividend yield, the fee absorbs one half of the dividend income." He later stated, "Investors can't control returns offered by the U.S. and world markets. But the one thing they can control is fees paid to investment managers. The only way to ensure that you can enjoy top quartile investment returns is to choose investment funds that have bottom quartile expense ratios. And, of course, the quintessential low-expense instruments are broad-based, indexed mutual funds and ETFs." (bolding mine)

# CHAPTER EIGHT:
# Other Investment Risks

What other risks of investing are out there in the investment jungle?

As noted before a single stock is a part ownership in that company. The company may go bankrupt and go completely out of business. If all of your money is in one stock, you are at risk of losing all of your investment. As stated before, bonds are essentially legal loans of money to a company or country. The value of a bond from one company may lose all of its value if that company goes bankrupt and goes completely out of business. Bond holders of the bonds of certain countries lost all of their investment when those countries ceased to exist after World War I. A few municipalities in the United States have gone bankrupt in recent years and the bonds of these cities became worthless. Even utilities, once thought safe, may go bankrupt due to overwhelming liabilities.

I believe that many cities and states in the United States at this time would be declared bankrupt after a proper audit and proper accounting.

Why?

These cities and states have severely underfunded their pension plans. The payments to retired employees due from the pension plans are legal obligations. There is no way that these underfunded pension plans will ever be fully funded. The underfunded pension plans are financial ticking time bombs which may lead to bankruptcies of multiple cities and states in the United States. In addition, as noted earlier, the investment performance of most pension plans is poor. Investing in municipal bonds which was once the "gold standard" of "safe" investing is probably much riskier than currently acknowledged. More on the investing performance of pension funds ahead.

Here is a quote from the 2013 Berkshire Hathaway letter to shareholders written by Warren Buffet: "Local and state financial problems are accelerating, in large part because public entities promised pensions they couldn't afford. Citizens and public officials typically under-appreciated the gigantic financial tapeworm that was born when promises were made that conflicted with a willingness to fund them. Unfortunately, pension mathematics today remain a mystery to most Americans."

I repeat:

Municipal bonds are riskier than generally acknowledged.

The risk of loss of investment from bankruptcy of any one company, city, state or country is handled by diversification. There is a separate chapter on diversification later in this book. A number of the large financial companies now have mutual funds and exchange traded funds for stocks and bonds which have remarkably low cost and follow certain indexes. For example, the Dow Industrial Average covers thirty specifically chosen stocks. The S&P 500 covers the stocks of the 500 largest companies. The NASDAQ 100 covers stocks of the 100 largest companies listed on the NASDAQ stock exchange. The Russell 2000 covers the stocks of the smallest 2000 companies out of the largest 3000 companies. There are extended market index funds which cover much smaller companies. Finally, there are "total" market funds which cover the entire market.

These funds provide an easy and cheap way to diversify your investments.

Next type of risk.

The personal risk. This may be the biggest risk to your success as an investor. Who are you? What kinds of an investor are you?

Repeated surveys of large financial firms disclose that:

The "average" investor does six to eight percent worse than the market as a whole averaged over many years.

Why?

If you are an "average" investor, that is, if you act like the "average" investor, you will do worse than the market as a whole itself.

Why?

The average investor tends to buy more when things are exciting. Things are exciting when the market has already gone up a lot. Thus, the average investor has missed out on much of the rise in the market. The average investor jumps into a rising market late. The average investor tends to sell after stock market values have dropped. The average investor jumps out of a falling market late. In essence, the average investor tends to buy when values are up and sell when values are down.

To minimize the risk of being an average investor, you have to act differently than the "average" investor.

You need to be a long time horizon buy and hold investor. You need to be an "investor' and not a "gambler."

Day trading and/or frequent buying and selling, as well as trying to time the market are gambling activities. On average, these activities will lower your long term investing results.

If you trade frequently, who are your opponents?

Recall, that for every buy and for every sell order, there is a person or company on the other side of the trade who thinks that they are making the right and clever move. Your opponents include computerized high-speed traders and professionals who spend all day studying companies, the world's economies and individual companies. They travel and meet with the various company executives.

Exactly why do you think you will be able to outsmart them?

I am told that the computerized high-speed traders pay money to place their computers closer to a main market's computer to obtain minute fractions of a second edge on the timing of their orders.

I repeat:

To "play" the market, that is to make frequent trades and/or try to time the stock market is gambling-plain and simple. You, an average investor, cannot hope to "outsmart" the market in the long run.

An investing strategy which is long term buy and hold with low cost United States stock index funds is not gambling, plain and simple. The overall stock market has risen over any twenty year time period in the past one hundred years.

**If the overall stock market has risen over any twenty year period in the past century, then a long term buy and hold strategy with low cost United States stock index funds is actually the SAFEST long term investment strategy you can find.**

That investment strategy has the best chance of you reaching your investment goals long term and you can do it without a financial manager. This is an example of an investment strategy which looks risky but is actually safer than other strategies.

There is obviously no guarantee the rise of the stock market will continue over the next one hundred years. However, no other investment option for the average passive investor presents itself as a better candidate for your investment strategy.

As I am writing this paragraph early in the morning on September 28, 2020, I need only look at the front page of The Wall Street Journal (WSJ) for an example to write about. I don't have to search for these examples! They're everywhere!

"**Investors** are betting on one of the most volatile U.S. election seasons on record, wagering on large swings in everything from stocks to currencies as they brace for what could be a weekslong haul of unpredictable events." (bolding mine)

This description of "**investors**" behavior is NOT, repeat NOT "investing" despite the WSJ reporter's use of the word "**investors**". This behavior is GAMBLING, pure and simple.

The net effect of this "investing" group behavior will be the transfer of wealth from some people or entities to other people or entities. This group behavior is a zero sum game. I ignore the small costs of actual "investing" behavior.

Definition:

"In game theory and economic theory. A zero-sum game is a mathematical representation of a situation in which each participant's gain or loss of utility is exactly balanced by the losses or gains of the utility of the other participants. If the total gains of the participants are added up and the total losses are subtracted, they will sum to zero." (Wikipedia, September 28, 2020)

For every buy and every sell in whatever markets you examine, there is a counter-party which (who) believes that they, the counter-party, are better, smarter and cleverer than you. I ignore the current low cost of buying and selling. Every buy and sell is a zero sum game in which what happens is, in effect, a simple transfer of wealth from one party to another. It depends who has overvalued or who has undervalued the asset. Again, I ignore the small costs of the actual "investing" behavior.

Another example. Another front page of The Wall Street Journal. September 25, 2020. Understand please! I don't have to search for these examples. They fall into my lap.

Headline: "Pension Funds Look to Increase Wagers On Stock Market." In the article the author states "**Pension funds and endowments have been shifting away from the U.S. stock market for years.** Some are now reconsidering that decision." And a few paragraphs later, "But pensions have been largely moving away from stocks in recent years, a shift that has hurt performance. The median public pension fund managing at least $1 billion had 46.6% of its portfolio in equities, as of June 30, with just a **21.3% allocation to U.S. equities**, according to data analytics provider, InvestmentMetrics LLC. By contrast, in 2013, the oldest data available, these funds had invested 52.7% of their portfolio in stocks, with 32.1% in U.S. shares." (bolding mine)

Stop! Reread the last paragraph. Think about this! Understand this! Don't read this quickly! Absorb this!

These gigantic, gargantuan and otherwise large pension funds are engaging in "risk" management by "extensive" diversification." Their investments in U.S. stocks over the past seven years have varied between 32% and 21% with a recent downward trend.

Consider this carefully! Ponder this!

**These large pension funds have "avoided" investing in stock equities in the most stable and most prosperous country in the world!**

I repeat:

These large pension funds have "avoided" investing in stock equities in the most stable and most prosperous country in the world!

Why?

**Following the "holy grail" of "risk management" by extensive diversification.**

Following the "holy grail" of minimizing the day to day volatility in the fervent belief that this minimizes "risk." Even when the long-term result of this behavior is long term inferior investing results. The "experts" are engaging in this "risk management" behavior thinking this is "proper" investing behavior. More, much, much more about this in the chapter, "My Critique of Modern Portfolio Theory."

Think about this carefully:

These pension funds have seriously underperformed when contrasted with investments in United States low cost stock index mutual funds over the same time period.

Think about this carefully:

**If the experts managing the investing of multiple billions of dollars are significantly underperforming United States low cost stock index mutual funds with their investment strategy, then YOU truly need to advance to becoming "your own teacher" in making your own investment decisions.**

As I stated in the preface, my goal in this book is to allow you to reach a comfort level that allows you to become your own investment manager.

So what other risks are out there?

Hubris!!!

Definition:

"Hubris describes a personality quality of extreme or foolish pride or dangerous overconfidence, often in combination with (or synonymous with) arrogance." (Wikipedia, September 28, 2020)

Avoiding hubris, avoiding overconfidence is essential to successful investing long term!

One other type of risk is your personal decisions regarding what to invest in and where to invest. You can decide poorly. You can decide poorly in an infinite number of ways.

What are some of them?

You can give your money to someone to invest for you and lose it all to fraud. This happened to the investors who gave their money to Bernie Madoff. Con men can be remarkably smooth and believable.

I wish to discuss the issue of transparency or more important the issue of **lack of transparency** in many investments.

Any "asset" which is not sold on the open market with high volume, like simple stocks, has the clear and present risk of lack of transparency. Even buying a "simple" bond is not simple. That one specific bond is not sold on the open market at high volume. Unless you are knowledgeable in the financial mathematics of evaluating the value of a specific bond, you cannot know the actual calculated value of that bond. You have to evaluate the risk of default for the bond. The bond provides an income stream for a certain period of time. Net present value types of calculations are used to try to assess the value of that bond. If you do not know how to do this, then this bond lacks transparency. You cannot quickly and easily assess the value of that bond. You are trusting someone else to tell you the value.

**When an investment lacks transparency, we again wander into the realm of moral hazard and the principal-agent problem.**

The financial world is filled with "exciting" assets which are not transparent. It sometimes seems that the less transparent a financial product is, the more exciting it is. For any of these complex financial instruments, you may not know exactly what you are buying. Let me rephrase that. It is not that you "may" not know what you are buying. It is essentially guaranteed that you will not know what you are buying.

If these complex financial assets are not transparent, you can take it as a guarantee that it is impossible to truly know what they are worth.

Here is a perfect example of "**lack of transparency**":

Consider the "mortgage backed securities" which were "all the rage" before the crash of 2008. In retrospect, these mortgage backed securities were filled with 0% down payment, no documentation required mortgages. These mortgages defaulted in large numbers leading to massive losses to owners of these securities. There was no transparency. Investors bought them on the advice of their financial managers and financial advisors much to their later chagrin.

**If you invest in low cost all United States stock index mutual funds, you are, in essence, investing in and betting on the health of the United States economy going forward. That is as transparent as you can get.**

You are guessing that the overall health of the United States economy going forward these next multiple decades is the "best bet" out there. There is no guarantee that the United States economy will continue to do well. However, there is the transparency that you know you are betting on the overall health of the United States economy.

As I have stated before, I don't need to search for examples of "bad" investments. They fall into my lap. Here are more examples of investments that suffered from a **lack of transparency**. Here are two current ones which appeared in the Wall Street Journal as I was editing this section on lack of transparency.

First Example:
Wall Street Journal (October 19, 2020; Page A1) Headline: "Stress on New York Property Worries Mortgage Investors". The article states "debt backed by hotels and shops have fallen, new loans have slowed …. And the real estate industry bracing for a hard hit." In the next paragraph, "Investors watch New York closely because **Wall Street slices such loans up, packages them together into bonds and sells them to pension funds and asset managers world-wide.** Collapsing prices for loans backed by top-tier properties in the Big Apple …". (bolding mine)

Financiers in Wall Street made money packaging and selling these "financial instruments." Even the Wall Street Journal labelled these complex financial instruments, "**bonds**." I seriously doubt that anyone who bought these "**bonds**" really knew what they were buying. These financial instruments are not simple "**bonds**" in which you are, in essence, loaning money to a single entity, corporation or country. These are complex packages of multiple income streams from multiple properties. These complex packages are not transparent. Buy a **bond** from a company, say IBM, and you are able to try to evaluate the risk of bankruptcy of IBM. Buy a "**bond**" of this complexity and you are unable to evaluate the risk.

**A "bond" of this complexity may be bond-like, but to me, it is not a bond.**

By calling this complex financial instrument a **bond**, the Wall Street firms who packaged this deal were able to fool investors into buying it, thinking it was a **bond**. This **bond-like** investment had a marked "**lack of transparency**." Any and all complex financial instruments should be avoided. Yet, "pension funds and asset managers worldwide" bought them.

**Who can you trust?**

Second Example:
Wall Street Journal (October 20, 2020; Page B1) Headline: "Variation of ETF Burns Investors". In the article: "… lost more than $100,000 after getting trapped in a zombie investment product." and "An exchange-traded note that he bet against was delisted over the summer" and "A number of high-profile implosions have sapped investor demand for the products" and "ETNs are the more complex and riskier cousins of exchange-traded funds. Like ETFs they track the price of a basket of stocks, bonds or commodities, but they don't own the underlying assets they track. **Instead they are debt issued by a bank that matures by a certain date, similar to a corporate bond.**" (bolding mine)

The reporter for the Wall Street Journal actually wrote that these non-transparent complex financial instruments are "**similar to a corporate bond**." No! I'm sorry! They are not similar to a corporate bond. Corporate bonds are relatively transparent. You know the corporation. You know the cash flow. You know the interest rate on the bond. You know how much longer the bond will pay the cash flow. Normal corporate bonds do not turn into "zombie investment products." The very fact that they are described in the

Wall Street Journal as "similar to a corporate bond" indicates exactly how non-transparent they are. Even the Wall Street Journal reporter was fooled.

I cannot even try to explain these products to you. Financiers packaged and marketed these complex instruments. These financiers earned larges fees for this activity. These complex investment products suffered from a "lack of transparency!"

**Avoid any financial product which is complex.**

**Avoid any financial product which you do not understand.**

**Avoid any financial product which is not transparent.**

**Avoid any financial product which is not simple.**

Keep It Simple Stupid.

Don't invest in anything that is not transparent!

Don't invest in anything that you do not understand!

Don't invest in the newest, coolest, latest investment fad.

The financiers who put these instruments together make money from their fees. You, on the other hand, probably not so much?

Why do people buy this stuff?

**Who can you trust?**

I am going to move on to other risks.

I believe one of the most common risks is fear, fear of loss, fear of the unknown and simply put general anxiety with respect to any investment decision. Many (maybe all) financial firms, financial advisors and financial managers ask new clients to fill out a form in which the client states his or her "risk tolerance."

There is little or no education about risk. There is no education involving the difference between long term risk and short term risk because the financial advisors and financial managers do not even think about the difference.

Many investors correctly state that they are risk averse. At a result they are placed in portfolios with large percentages of bonds.

**These "safe" "low risk" portfolios are actually at "high risk" of failing to grow enough to meet long term net worth goals.**

It is strange.

It seems contradictory.

Yet:

**Utilizing a "safe," low risk," "conservative" investing strategy actually has a very "high-risk" of failing to meet long-term investing goals due to poor long term investing performance.**

I argue that:

**The actual, "real" risk of any portfolio or basket of assets changes with the investment time horizon. With a long time horizon, a portfolio with a high percentage of stocks is actually "safer" when comparing probable final investment results.**

By long time horizon, I mean a minimum of ten years and certainly twenty to fifty years.

Let's look at "risk" from another point of view.

I sometimes divide "investing risk" into two categories, which I call "known risk" and "unknown risk." In my classification, you can control the "known risks" but you can't control the "unknown risks."

In my classification, the "known risks" include allowing your cost of investing to be too high, putting too much of your assets in bonds, excessive diversification in lower performing assets, buying high and selling low, that is excitement buying after the market has gone up and panic selling after the market has gone down, being afraid to invest and keeping your money in cash.

From a statistician's point of view these are not "risks."

From my point of view:

These "known risks" are psychological risks or investor behavioral risks. I believe that more investors do poorly from these "known risks" than from "unknown risks."

What are the "unknown risks." Everything else. Looking for the "unknown risks" is like looking at an old map and seeing an unknown area marked, "Here be monsters." These unknown risks include black swan pandemics, bioterror, the four horsemen of death, famine, war and conquest, social unrest, cultural suicide, political societal upheaval and possible dystopic futures of infinite varieties. There are societal upheavals sufficiently severe that no amount of planning can protect against them. You, the reader, need to accept this. You need to ignore this as much as is humanly possible. You need get on with your life.

Investing, particularly investing for the long term, requires an optimistic approach to life.

What have other people said?

From the Wall Street Journal (April 22, 2009, article by Sam Mamudi) Headline: "Managed Funds Take Beating From Indexes". The article begins, "Investors in actively managed mutual funds for the past five years have reason to wonder what they have been paying for: a new study from Standard and Poor's finds that **70% of large-cap fund managers who use the S&P 500-stock index as a benchmark for comparison have failed to match the performance of the index over that time.**" Later in the article: "**The failure of active management is replicated across almost all categories, not only U.S. stock funds but also bond funds and even emerging-market funds.**" Later in the article: "**We consistently see that once you extend time horizons to five years, the majority of active managers are behind their benchmarks**," said Srikant Dash, global head of research and design at S&P." (bolding mine)

With respect to avoiding investments in complex, non-transparent entities, from the Wall Street Journal (November 30, 2011, Page C4), "Insurer Mariah Re Ltd is poised to default on a $100 million, three-year **bond** that it issued in November 2010 on behalf of American Mutual Family Insurance Co. with **bond holders expected to lose all of their principal**." The headline of this article was "First-Ever Securities to Cover Damage Exclusively From Severe Thunderstorms Are Poised to Default." (bolding mine)

Whatever these securities were, they were not **bonds**, despite the article describing the investors as "**bond holders**." What were these securities? They were complex, non-transparent financial instruments. The developers of these complex financial instruments earned high fees. The investors lost everything.

With respect to avoiding investing in the newest, coolest, latest investment fad. I find these examples all the time. From the Wall Street Journal, November 9, 2020, Page R1, The Section on "Investing in Funds and ETfs." … "Pick a theme, any theme, and there's probably a way to invest in it." … "There are more than 800 thematic funds in global markets with assets totaling more than $183 billion" … "The interest in thematic investments isn't hard to understand." ... "More interesting, that is, but usually not more lucrative." ... "Investors need to approach this category with a healthy degree of skepticism, given its track record."

**Avoid investments which are new!**

**Avoid investments which you do not understand!**

**Avoid investments which are complex!**

**Avoid investments which are not transparent!**

**Keep It Simple Stupid!**

Remember! The financial agents who sold these bonds made money on their fees. They probably did not lose money on the bond default. The sucker investors did.

From the Washington Post, James K. Glassman's last column (June 27, 1999, Page H1), "Stocks are investments for the long run, which by my definition is at least seven years. If you can't stay in stocks that long, stay out. In the short term stocks are very volatile (their prices fluctuate wildly), but in the long term, they are no more risky than Treasury bonds-and they return a lot more. In fact, stocks, for the long term investor, are a miraculous gift. If the averages of the past 200 years hold, you can double your money in 6 ½ years and barely lift a finger."

Now on to my "Critique of Modern Portfolio Theory."

# CHAPTER NINE:
# My Critique of Modern Portfolio Theory

In the preface to this book I mentioned that I planned to explain in simple terms why I believe that the basic investing theory (Modern Portfolio Theory) used by financial advisors and financial managers is flawed. I stated that I planned to discuss why I believe following this theory results in sub-optimal long term investing results. I stated that I would explain what I consider to be the major flaws in the financial advice and financial management provided by most financial advisors and financial managers.

As I stated earlier, I have set myself a high bar. Here goes.

At the beginning of Chapter One, I discussed in general terms the fact that people often assume that they are able to calculate risks in situations in which it is not possible to calculate the risks. I stated that if a theory starts with a false assumption, then the math that follows that false assumption may give results which appear to be correct, however the act of making the false assumption means that any calculation based on the false assumption will inevitably lead to incorrect results.

Economists have expended intensive effort trying to measure and quantify the risk of investments using mathematical and statistical techniques. If you look at the value of a stock, the value of a bond, the value of a mixture of different stocks, the value of a mixture of different bonds, the value of a mixture of different stocks and bonds or the value of any basket of assets, the total value of your basket of assets may vary by the fraction of a second, by the minute, by the hour, by the day, etc. Each buy and each sell, anywhere in the world, of each asset you hold in your basket of assets may occur at a different price than the one before. Each change in price of one of the assets in the basket of assets will result in a different total valuation of the entire basket of assets.

The day to day variation or variability of the total value of any asset or basket of assets is often called volatility.

A mathematical term called the standard deviation of the day to day volatility of a specific basket of assets is often used when people attempt to quantify or measure the size of the volatility. The greater the volatility, the greater the standard deviation of that volatility. It is not necessary for you to know what a standard deviation is. Simply put, it is a method which measures the magnitude of the day to day variation in the total value of your basket of assets.

**It is assumed as truth in Modern Portfolio Theory that the day to day variation (volatility) in the total value of your basket of assets is an "actual," "correct," "proper," "real" measure of the risk of investing in your basket of assets. It is assumed as truth that investments with greater day to day volatility (higher beta) have a probability of greater investment return. Similarly, it is accepted as truth that any basket of assets with a higher day to day volatility is of higher risk than a basket of assets with lower day to day volatility.**

These are the basic assumptions of the Modern Portfolio Theory. Are they true?

Historically, it is true that stocks prices have been more volatile than bond prices.

Historically, it is true that in the long term stocks have performed better than bonds.

Historically, it is true that in any portfolio mix of stocks and bonds, the portfolio with more stocks has had greater volatility and has also had better performance over time. This is a correlation. Many assume that there is causation between the greater volatility and better investment performance. Is this true?

**Modern Portfolio Theory equates lower day to day volatility of a basket of assets with greater safety (i.e. lower risk).**

Consider:

**The day to day volatility of the value of your basket of assets is a short term phenomenon.**

**Safety with respect to long term investing results is a long term phenomenon.**

**Modern Portfolio Theory equates the short term safety of the lower volatility of a basket of assets with long term safety!**

Is this true?

Many financial advisors and financial managers recommend a combination of stocks and bonds. Often the advisors recommend 50-60% stocks and 40-50% bonds for an individual investor's basket of assets regardless of the investor's time horizon.

Where do these percentages come from?

Modern Portfolio Theory posits that the standard deviation of the volatility of your basket of assets is the actual measure of risk regardless of the investment time horizon. If you accept Modern Portfolio Theory's definition of risk, then graphs of what is called the **"efficient frontier" show that a mixture of stocks and bonds with 50-60% stocks and 40-50% bonds historically optimizes the best expected return consistent with a given level of risk.** The exact per cent combination will vary somewhat depending on what data is used in calculating the day to day volatility.

The section on Modern Portfolio Theory in Wikipedia (August 13, 2020) states that "Modern portfolio theory or mean-variance analysis is **a mathematical framework for assembling a portfolio of assets such that the expected return is maximized for a given level of risk**. It is a formalization and extension of diversification in investing, the idea that owning different kinds of financial assets is less risky than owning only one type." (bolding mine) The developers of this theory were awarded the Nobel prize.

Let me repeat part of the description of Modern Portfolio Theory.

**Modern Portfolio Theory is a "mathematical framework for assembling a portfolio of assets such that the expected return is maximized for a given level of risk."**

If the standard deviations of the day to day volatility for different baskets of assets (different fractions of stocks and bonds) are graphed versus the "expected return," an "efficient frontier" may be calculated and graphed. Per Wikipedia (August 13, 2020) "the **efficient frontier** (or portfolio frontier) is an investment portfolio which occupies the 'efficient' parts of the risk-return spectrum. **It is the set of portfolios which satisfy the condition that no other portfolio exists with a higher expected return but with the same standard deviation of return (i.e. the risk.)**" (bolding mine)

Underlying all of this is the "**efficient market hypothesis**." Per Wikipedia (August 13, 2020) "The efficient-market hypothesis is a hypothesis in financial economics that states that asset prices reflect all available information. A direct implication is that it is **impossible** to 'beat the market' consistently on a risk-adjusted basis since market prices should only react to new information." (bolding is mine)

For those of you interested, there is extensive literature concerning these concepts. I am not presenting these concepts and theories in any more detail. I do not plan to delve into the mathematical complexities of Modern Portfolio Theory. My concern is the basic assumptions of Modern Portfolio Theory.

My concern regarding Modern Portfolio Theory is that the "risk" of any basket of assets is defined and accepted as the standard deviation of the "day to day" volatility of the portfolio of assets regardless of investment time horizon.

I repeat: "regardless of investment time horizon".

If you are placed in the arbitrary situation in which you are required to invest in a basket of assets and then may be unexpectedly told to liquidate your basket of assets without warning, sometime in the next few days or weeks, then the standard deviation of the day to day volatility of that basket of assets "may" be a reasonable valuation of the risk of that investment. That is a hypothetical situation. That is not real life. If you cannot leave your money in an investment for at least five years and preferably ten years, you should not invest that money, but keep it in cash-like investments.

What happens if your time horizon is ten, twenty, thirty, forty, fifty years or more?

**Does the day to day volatility of your basket of assets (as your measure of risk) have any correlation with the expected return on investment with that long of a time horizon?**

I repeat:

What happens if your time horizon is ten, twenty, thirty, forty, fifty years or more?

Does the day to day volatility of your basket of assets (as your measure of risk) have any correlation with the expected return on investment with that long of a time horizon?

My answer is a loud and definitive NO!

Why do I believe this?

Let's look at some examples.

Example One:
Per Wikipedia (August 13, 2020), The Dow Jones Industrial Average was established on May 26, 1896. The first Dow Jones Industrial Average included the General Electric Company.

Questions:

Did the standard deviation of the day to day volatility of the General Electric Company stock in June 1896 have any correlation with the value of General Electric stock on August 1, 1929, a month or so before the stock market crash of 1929?

Did the standard deviation of the day to day volatility of the General Electric Company stock in June 1896 have any correlation with the value of General Electric stock in 1930, in the year after the big crash?

Did the standard deviation of the day to day volatility of the General Electric Company stock in June 1896 have any correlation with the value of General Electric stock in August 2020?

The obvious answer to me is NO to all three questions.

**It makes no sense that the day to day jiggling of the price of a single stock (a short term phenomenon) has any correlation with its stock price thirty to a hundred years later (a long term phenomenon).**

Seriously, commonsense will tell you that.

The obvious answer to me is that:

**The standard deviation of the day to day volatility of any individual stock or any basket of assets has little to no correlation with the value of that stock ten years later. Much less twenty, thirty, forty or fifty years later.**

Example Two:
Per Wikipedia (August 14, 2020), the ten biggest corporation bankruptcies in United States history include Lehman Brothers Holdings, Inc., Washington Mutual, Worldcom, Inc., General Motors, CIT Group, Enron Corp., Consenco, Inc., MF Global, Chrysler and Thornburg Mortgage. These ten largest bankruptcies all occurred between 2001 and 2011.

I argue that the standard deviation of the volatility of a basket of the stocks which contained these ten corporations and only these ten corporations in 1998 had absolutely zero correlation with the "risk" of investing in these ten corporations in 1998.

I argue that the standard deviation of the volatility of a basket of the stocks of these ten corporations and only these ten corporations in 1998 had absolutely zero correlation with the "risk" that all ten of these corporations would declare bankruptcy within the next thirteen years.

**It seems clear to me that the Market Portfolio Theory's risk measure of day to day volatility does not reflect real life risk regarding firms in distress due to fraud, mismanagement, bad business decisions and general economic distress for any long time horizon**

So, how much of a correlation is there actually between the day to day volatility of a basket of assets and the actual, real time, real life risk of the investment particularly with a time horizon between ten and fifty years? I argue none.

Recall that no one in September 2019 predicted a severe pandemic in 2020. The severe economic downturn due to the pandemic, the extensive business shutdown and the general fear were not predictable. As I am writing this, companies are going bankrupt as the result of this economic downturn. The timing of this "black swan" event was not predictable.

**I submit that the day to day volatility of the stocks of these companies last year has no correlation with the fact that they are going bankrupt this year because of the pandemic.**

If this be true, then it follows that:

**If there is little or no correlation between the day to day volatility of your basket of assets and the risk/return probability in a future ten to fifty years out, then the sophisticated mathematics of the Modern Portfolio Theory offers no useful real world information regarding any risk/return calculation regarding your basket of assets if your time horizon is ten to fifty years.**

**I argue that the day to day volatility of a basket of assets provides zero information regarding the risk of investing in this basket of assets, if you have a ten to fifty year time horizon.**

**If the volatility of the day to day valuation of a basket of assets is not a valid measure of actual, real life investment risk for a time horizon of ten**

**to fifty years, then the mathematical results of Modern Portfolio Theory should not be used for long term investing decisions.**

If this be true, then the use of the "efficient frontier" in determining the optimal mix of stocks and bonds leads to intellectually satisfying, mathematically precise and psychologically comforting results. Unfortunately, these results are wrong when investing with a long term horizon.

So, why do so many financial advisors and managers stick with the results of Modern Portfolio Theory? Obviously, I don't know. Part of the reason may be the psychology of herd mentality. If everyone else is doing it, I should too. If I do what everyone else is doing, I can't be blamed if my investment results are not optimal. Perhaps many or most are not as thoughtful and skeptical as they should be.

Another thought:

**Following Modern Portfolio Theory leads to extensive diversification in order to minimize day to day volatility.**

The investing time horizon for financial advisors and financial managers is days to weeks to perhaps one month. Your personal investing time horizon should be a minimum of ten years and possibly as long as fifty years.

Why?

What is the motivation of the portfolio managers of your personal investments, of the portfolio managers of large pension funds and of the portfolio managers of large university endowments?

If the value of the managed portfolio (your private portfolio, the pension fund portfolio, the university endowment portfolio) drops too much, too quickly, the client will pull the assets away from the financial manager or financial advisor.

All financial advisors and financial managers are constantly worried about the short term volatility of the value of the basket of assets they are managing.

How do these financial advisors and financial managers handle their concern regarding short term volatility of the investments under their management? Extensive diversification among multiple asset classes decreases the magnitude of the day to day volatility of any basket of assets. Extensive diversification among multiple asset classes minimizes short term volatility. Minimizing short term volatility helps to protect the financial managers from large, short term volatility events!

Consider this:

**Extensive diversification into multiple assets classes will involve investing in asset classes that perform poorly when compared with the long term results of the United States stock market.**

If this be true, then extensive diversification among multiple asset classes does not decrease your overall risk if your investing horizon is ten, twenty or fifty years.

In fact, it follows that:

**Extensive diversification will lower your long term investing results.**

In fact, it follows that:

**If extensive diversification lowers your long term investing results, then extensive diversification is not "safe" when considering whether you will reach your long term investing goals.**

Of all of the asset classes recommended for maximum diversification, which asset class has done the best over any twenty to fifty year time period over the past one hundred years? United States stocks! End of discussion. United

States stocks! Over the long term, value stocks have done a little better than growth stocks and small capitalization stocks have done a little better than large capitalization stocks. For almost every ten-year period in the past century stocks have outperformed bonds. The rare time bonds outperformed stocks over ten years, it was by about one percent.

Consider:

The largest daily changes in the S&P Stock Index (Wikipedia, 8/14/20) have been 16.61% up on March 15, 1933 and 20.47% down on October 19, 1987.

The day to day variation in an all stock portfolio can be truly mind numbingly, panic strickenly awful.

If you are going to invest in a long term buy and hold investment strategy with low cost United States stock index mutual funds, then

**YOU HAVE TO BE PREPARED TO RIDE OUT THE INEVITABLE, OCCASIONAL HORRIFIC RAPID DROPS IN VALUE WITHOUT SELLING.**

**ARE YOU ABLE TO DO THAT?**

**IF NOT, MY ADVICE IS NOT APPROPRIATE FOR YOU!**

Here is an example of following Modern Portfolio Theory.

As I am writing this sentence on September 15, 2020, one headline in the Business and Finance section of the Wall Street Journal (WSJ) states "Bond Yields Encourage Risk Taking." The second paragraph states, "Real yields are what you get on U.S. government bonds after compensating for inflation, and are typically associated with the yields on Treasury inflation-protected securities, or TIPS. Right now those aren't just low, they are negative." The next paragraph states "At the current rate, if you buy ordinary 10-year Treasury notes, you can expect to lose roughly a dollar for every $100 you own."

Please reread the above paragraph several times and digest exactly what it says.

Are you blown away by this Wall Street Journal article presented in such a matter of fact fashion?

I was!

Think about it and continue reading.

Inflation, at this time, is very low. This WSJ article states that at this time (September 15, 2020), if you buy "**safe**" 10-year U.S. treasury notes you are essentially **guaranteed to lose money**.

Let me repeat:

Inflation, at this time, is very low. If you buy "**safe**" 10-year U.S. treasury notes you are essentially **guaranteed to lose money**.

Ask yourself, "Does this make any sense? Does it make any sense to invest in an investment almost guaranteed to lose money?

My answer is a loud and clear, "NO!"

Have you read in the news that the U.S. government was unable to sell 10-year U.S. treasury notes? I sure didn't! That means a lot of people, a lot of institutions and a lot of pension funds among others were buying these "safe' U.S. Treasury notes which were almost guaranteed to lose money.

Why? Why? Why? Why? Why?

I think five "Whys" are enough.

Let's look at this from another point of view.

When the U.S. government sells a 10-year treasury note, it is in effect borrowing that money from the purchaser of the 10-year treasury note for ten years. To summarize, the Wall Street Journal was reporting that:

The United States government is currently able to borrow large sums of money for an interest rate so low that the entities loaning the money to the U.S. government are almost guaranteed to lose money over the next ten years.

Please allow me to emphasize that the "almost guarantee of a loss" does not allow for the possibility of inflation rising during the next ten years leading to even greater losses for the buyers of these 10 year treasury notes.

**TALK ABOUT A RISKY INVESTMENT!**

**THIS INVESTMENT IS SO RISKY THAT IT IS ALMOST GUARANTEED TO LOSE MONEY!**

Yet, these experts, these financial gurus, these financial advisors, these financial managers, these pension fund managers, these international financiers think that this is a good and "SAFE" investment.

Am I missing something here or does this suggest that the financial world is just a little bit crazy? Obviously, I think I am right. You, the reader, have to decide where the craziness lies.

Question:

Why are so many entities and people buying these 10-year U.S. treasury notes? Why are so many entities and people buying 10-year U.S. treasury notes which are almost guaranteed to lose money?

Answer:

They are doing this for "safety."

Why is this investing behavior considered "safe?"

Modern Portfolio theory dogma insists (mathematically) that it is "safest" to lower the day to day volatility of your total portfolio.

Financial managers and financial advisors have the incentive to lower the day to day volatility of your total portfolio to minimize the "risk" that you will withdraw your money from their advice and management if the value of your portfolio drops too much within a short period of time.

Following Modern Portfolio Theory and minimizing the day to day volatility of your basket of assets results in the buying of these almost guaranteed losing investments in order to lower the day to day volatility of the total portfolio. Modern Portfolio Theory determines that this investing behavior (buying an almost guaranteed loss) results in lowering the "risk" of the total portfolio.

I ask:

**How does buying a guaranteed losing investment provide safety if your investing time horizon is ten to fifty years?**

I ask again:

**How does buying a guaranteed losing investment provide safety if your investing time horizon is ten to fifty years?**

My answer:

"It doesn't."

I mean really!

Does it make any sense to you at all that buying a losing investment makes your basket of assets safer?

Let me repeat:

Does it make any sense to you at all that buying a losing investment makes your basket of assets safer?

I argue that:

This investing behavior is senseless, if you are investing for ten to fifty years.

I repeat:

This investing behavior is senseless, if you are investing for ten to fifty years.

If your investing time horizon is hours to days to weeks to a few years, you have no business investing your money in anything but cash-like investments anyway.

Some buyers of these notes may be international investors seeking "safety" in U.S. securities. Some buyers of these notes may be willing to accept a "small" guaranteed loss because they fear other investments will have a worse outcome. If your time horizon is "short" that may well be true. If your time horizon is "long" that decision suffers, I believe, from, shall I call it, "short-term-sightedness." Some buyers may be pension funds. More on this below.

What are the results of following the religion of Modern Portfolio Theory?

Let's look at CalPERS.

CalPERS is the California Public Employees' Retirement System. CalPERS is responsible for investing the pension contributions for the public employees of the state of California. From "The Sacramento Bee" newspaper: CalPERS reached $400 billion dollars under management on January 17, 2020. From the calpers.ca.gov website: On September 20, 2020 the total fund performance for the 20-year time period was 5.5%. For the thirty-year time period the fund returned an average of 8.0% annually.

From the wealthsimple.com website: On September 30, 2020, the following are the 20 and 30-year average yearly returns for certain stock indices as of June 30, 2020.

20-year returns
S & P 500                                               9.90%
Dow Jones Industrial Average           7.03%
Russell 2000                                        7.70%

30-year returns
Dow Jones Industrial Average           10.99%
Russel 2000                                         9.29%

Let's compare the 20-year performance.

The 20-year performance for CalPERS which manages approximately $400 billion was 5.5%. The other plain, vanilla, ordinary U.S. stock indices for 20 years showed a yearly average gain of 9.90%, 7.03% and 7.70%.

Which did better?

**NOT CalPERS.**

Remember the difference in the average yearly return is compounded over the twenty year period. Recall that the longer the time horizon the greater the final difference due to compounding. Recall that earlier I showed that a 2% difference over fifty years leads to an investment result less than half of what it would have been with a 2% greater yearly return over that period of time.

Let's compare the thirty-year performance.

The 30-year performance for CalPERS which manages approximately $400 billion was 8.0%. The plain, vanilla, ordinary stock indices for 30 years showed a yearly average gain of 10.99% and 9.29%.

Which did better?

**NOT CalPERS.**

Remember the difference in the average yearly return is compounded over thirty years. Recall that the longer the time horizon the greater the final difference.

In order to maintain some reason when discussing this, I include the maximum losses in 2008 for these stock indices.

In 2008, there were temporary, huge, massive, stupendous, frightening losses in these indices!

S & P 500 -**37.00%**
Dow Jones Industrial Average -**31.93%**
Russell 2000 -**33.79%**

Why am I including this list of 2008 losses for these stock indices?

I include the 2008 temporary losses in the stock indices to reflect and emphasize that an all stock investment program will include the occasional episode of massive, rapid but temporary loss.

The road to success is to "ignore" these episodes and refrain from panic selling.

Back to CalPERS.

Why has CalPERS underperformed the plain, vanilla, ordinary stock indices?

The CalPERS website contains an extensive wordy description (almost 100 pages) of their investment philosophy. From the website on October 1, 2020, here are a few quotes:

"The assets of CalPERS will be **broadly diversified to minimize the effect of short-term losses within any investment program**." (bolding mine)

"CalPERS recognizes that over 90% of the variation in investment returns of a large, **well diversified pool of assets** can typically be attributed to asset allocation decisions. **The performance objective is to achieve positive active asset allocation returns over rolling five year periods**." (bolding mine)

"Adherence to the asset class policy ranges approved by the Committee, with any **rebalancing** being performed efficiently and prudently;" (bolding mine)

"Criteria for consideration when evaluating an asset class shall include the following: Strategic role of the asset class in the **asset liability management (ALM) framework based on fundamental characteristics and risk and return drivers**." (bolding mine)

"Further, the asset class must have a basis for developing expected investment returns, risks, and correlations for the purpose of financial study."

I could add more quotes from the approximately hundred-page document available to all online. I wish to emphasize, in the quotes I have provided, the CalPERS investment philosophy is centered around the basic tenets of Modern Portfolio Theory, namely: minimizing short term losses, the use of a large, well diversified pool of assets, rebalancing and a framework based on fundamental risk and return drivers.

The entire CalPERS document pays homage to Modern Portfolio Theory.

What has been the result of CalPERS following Modern Portfolio Theory with its emphasis on extensive diversification, minimizing short term volatility and, rebalancing between multiple arbitrary asset classes? This $400 billion-dollar pension fund staffed with financial experts has underperformed simple, plain vanilla all stock index funds over the past 20 and 30-year time periods by 2-4% per year margins. Remember that the yearly 2-4% difference compounds over long time horizons.

Again, I repeat:

Why has CalPERS underperformed the plain, vanilla stock indices?

Because they are following the religion of Modern Portfolio Theory. For the past 20 and 30-year time periods, you, a simple, ordinary, plain vanilla investor could have outperformed this $400 billion dollar behemoth with all of its "expertise."

How could you, "an ordinary investor" have beaten the results of CalPERS?

Simple!

If you had used an "easy" long term buy and hold strategy with low cost United States stock index mutual funds or ETFs, coupled with avoiding panic selling during massive downturns.

I wish to emphasize my last sentence.

**I wish to emphasize again the importance of avoiding panic selling during massive downturns.**

There are other reasons CalPERS and other public pension funds underperform. These public pension funds may be restricted by law in what investments they may utilize. Historically, many were limited to bonds or just municipal bonds. In addition, there is constant oversight by the state legislators. No short term significant loss is tolerated by the state legislators. No short-term loss is tolerated by public opinion.

**The politics of running a public pension fund requires careful attention to short term volatility.**

The same is probably true for managing a university endowment fund. If short term volatility is not acceptable, then these public pension funds and university endowments will utilize excessive diversification to minimize short term volatility. This use of excessive diversification, as discussed above, will lead to suboptimal results going forward. The use of excessive diversification to minimize short term volatility by the public pension funds and university endowments is similar to the motivations of ALL financial advisors and ALL financial managers.

**This further underscores the necessity for you to become your own financial manager if you desire best investment results for yourself.**

Unfortunately, poor management has also been as issue at CalPERS. From Forbes (June 29, 2015) "America's largest public pension plan—had earlier this year surprisingly stated that it did not know how much it was paying some of its highest-cost Wall Street private equity money managers."

I repeat:

Yearly investment cost is a major factor in determining final investment results long-term.

Avoiding the extensive diversification which results in investing in lower performing assets is a major factor in determining final investment results long term.

From Forbes (June 29, 2015) "The annualized rate of return on its (CalPERS) hedge fund investments over the last 10 years was 4.8%" Picking poor investments will certainly harm long-term investment results.

You, as an individual investor, have the ability:

**to avoid excessive diversification**

**to avoid high yearly costs**

**to avoid picking poor investments**

**to outperform the pension fund managers**

**by sticking to low cost all United States stock index mutual funds with one of the large financial firms.**

As I have explained above, the public pension funds, the financial managers, the financial advisors and the Registered Investment Advisors will not achieve this.

You, as an individual investor, will hopefully be able to ignore short term volatility in the interest of better long-term investing results.

The main issue:

**CAN YOU AVOID PANIC SELLING IN TIMES OF SEVERE ECONOMIC DISTRESS?**

I repeat:

Understand why I emphasize that you need to become your own "teacher", why you need to "keep it simple stupid", why you need to make your own decisions and why high yearly costs and excessive diversification in the pursuit of decreased short term volatility will lead to suboptimal results.

There are clearly other ways to invest. If you have time to spend and the ability to repair and rehabilitate houses and rental apartments, investing in real estate can be successful. This book is not written for these people. Repairing, rehabilitating and renting real estate is active investing. I am not writing for that type of investor. I am writing for the average "passive" investor.

Whatever you invest in: Keep It Simple Stupid. What is simple? Investing in low cost United States stock mutual funds run by the large financial firms is simple.

Up until now my argument against the use of the Modern Portfolio Theory has been a commonsense opinion that it does not make sense that the use of the day to day volatility of a basket of assets as a measure of risk has any correlation with the value of that basket of assets ten to fifty years into the future. I have bolstered that argument with the example of a stock which has been in existence for over one hundred years, namely General Electric. I have also raised the question that the day to day volatility of a specific stock seems to have little correlation with the probability of that specific corporation going bankrupt in the next decade. I also questioned whether the day to day volatility of many companies in the year before the pandemic had any correlation with the risk of those companies going bankrupt due to the economic dislocation of the 2020 pandemic.

I wish to continue my critique of Modern Portfolio Theory from another point of view.

The past one hundred to one hundred and twenty years of stock and bond market experience has shown the following:

1. It is a fact that stocks are more volatile that bonds.
2. It is a fact that over long periods of time stocks have significantly and continually out performed bonds.

3. The two points above demonstrate a strong correlation between more volatile assets and greater investment performance when stocks are compared with bonds.
4. Is this just a correlation? Is there some underlying causation connecting the higher volatility of stocks and the higher performance of stocks? Modern Portfolio Theory seems to posit that there is a causal connection between the higher volatility and higher investment performance.
5. Why do stocks outperform bonds?
6. Why are stocks more volatile than bonds?
7. Let me return to the "efficient market hypothesis. I repeat: Per Wikipedia (8/13/20) "The efficient-market hypothesis is a hypothesis in financial economics that states that asset prices reflect all available information. A direct implication is that it is impossible to 'beat the market' consistently on a risk-adjusted basis since market prices should only react to new information."
8. Are the stock and bond markets equally "efficient? I argue that the stock market is relatively "inefficient" when compared with the bond market. With the internet there exists rapid spread of information. The veracity of this information is always suspect. But even with equality of information, the ability to judge the value of the stock of any specific corporation is extraordinarily difficult. Actually, the ability to judge the value of the stock of any specific corporation ten or twenty years in the future is impossible. For example, look at Apple. Its continuing success is dependent on the next "big" product. In the next twenty years, in the next fifty years, how will Apple perform. Truly, nobody knows.

Thus, even if there is "efficiency" in obtaining information about individual corporations, there is no "efficiency" in interpreting that information. Even if there is "efficiency" in obtaining information, there is no "efficiency" in predicting a corporation's future ten to fifty years into the future. I argue that there is marked "inefficiency" in attempting to judge "value" in the stock market. I argue that the appearance of "efficiency" within the stock market is an "illusion". I argue that there is significant "inefficiency" in judging value in the stock market particularly with long time horizons.

In every year there are corporations whose stock skyrockets and others whose stock plummets like a "falling knife." Similar to horse racing everybody seems to be backing a different horse. Except in the stock market there are thousands of horses racing, not just eight or twelve. So many "investors" are trying to find that one stock which will skyrocket for them. So many investors hear of the "winners" who have been "lucky" and like gamblers think, "that could have been me" and will be me next year.

9. I argue that, in contrast, the bond market is actually much more "efficient" than the stock market. The main unknowns for evaluating the value of bonds are the stability of the corporations or governments issuing the bonds and the prediction of future interest rates. The cash flow of the bond is known and will continue as long as the entity which sold the bond continues to exist. The cash flow from a bond does not change if a corporation does well or poorly as long as that corporation remains sufficiently healthy that investors do not perceive a risk of bankruptcy.

Take for example a 30 year United States treasury bond that I just purchased today. What will its value be in 20 years? The math used to calculate the answer is not controversial. There is no serious concern that the United States will have ceased to exist before 20 years has elapsed. The only arguable unknown in the calculation is the prediction regarding what the interest rates will be for the next twenty years. Contrast the question regarding the value of the U.S. bond in twenty years with the question, what will the value of a share of Apple stock be in twenty years? Truly completely and utterly unknown. There are far fewer unknowns when evaluating the value of a bond.

I argue that the difference in volatility between the stock market and the bond market is due to the marked difference in "efficiency" in valuing stocks and bonds. I argue that the decreased "efficiency" in valuing stocks versus bonds leads to the greater volatility in investor behavior in the stock market.

10. Why has the stock market outperformed the bond market over long periods of time? I argue that bonds have been touted as "safe" investments for so long (clearly over a century), that large numbers of investors are willing to buy bonds regardless of the interest paid, regardless of the future expected investment performance. I argue that large numbers of investors are willing to accept lower long term investment returns from bonds because they have been convinced this is "safe" investing behavior. I argue that the bond market is a seller's market because the sellers of bonds are able to borrow money at remarkably low interest rates. I argue that stocks outperform bonds because investors seriously and profoundly under price bonds as they scramble for the assumed safety of bonds.

I argue that the better performance of stocks with respect to bonds is not due to the greater volatility of stocks, but due to the prolonged and persistent under pricing of bonds due to their perceived greater safety.

11. Reprise: I argue that the higher volatility of the stock market is the result of investor behavior which results from inefficiency in valuing stocks. I argue that the increased volatility results from so many people trying to find the mother lode, the holy grail, the fountain of youth, that is, the one stock or several stocks which will skyrocket. The higher volatility of the stock market results from the behavior of the "gamblers" namely the frequent buyers and sellers. These investor behaviors cause the greater volatility in the performance of individual stocks. I argue that the greater volatility of stocks when compared with bonds is due to the difficulty, the "inefficiency" of valuing corporations going forward. I argue that the greater performance of the stock market is not causally related to the increased volatility caused by investor behavior but simply correlated with it. I argue that the greater performance of the stock

market compared with the bond market is due to the prolonged under pricing of bonds because of their perceived safety.

12. Any study comparing baskets of assets of different percentages of stocks and bonds will always show the correlation between greater day to day volatility and better investing performance. I repeat: this is not the result of a causal connection between volatility and performance, but the result of a correlation caused by the difference in "market efficiency" between the stock market and the bond market which leads to the difference in "investor behavior" which results from those differential efficiencies and the persistent under pricing of bonds due to their perceived safety.

I argue that the "efficient frontier" of risk/return calculations is an illusion which assumes a causal connection between volatility and risk which is false.

13. People have been "trained" to buy bonds because they are "safe." Modern Portfolio Theory determines that bonds are "safe" because having bonds in the portfolio helps to lower day to day volatility. I argue that bonds have lower volatility because the bond market is more "efficient" than the stock market. That is, there is more agreement generally regarding the value of any specific bond.

I argue that the lower volatility of the bond market is not a sign of safety for long term investing but simply a sign of the greater efficiency of the bond market.

For any long term investing strategy, bonds are not safe with respect to an investor reaching that investor's long term investing performance goals because of bond's inferior long term performance.

14. My ideas should be testable by curious financial academicians. I repeat: Any study of volatility and performance which looks at mixtures of stocks and bonds will always find a correlation between volatility and

performance because stocks perform better than bonds and stocks have greater volatility due to investor behavior. I recommend that curious financial academicians randomly divide the entire stock market into groups of three, five, seven or other small number of stocks. Measure the day to day volatility for a randomly determined previous month for each randomly chosen group of stocks. Then examine the twenty year investment performance result for each group. Be sure to include stocks that have disappeared due to bankruptcy to avoid survivor bias. Include dividends from dividend paying stocks and reinvest the dividends in the same stock. Allow for stock mergers and cash purchases of stock. Look for any correlation between the short term volatility of the different randomly chosen groups and their twenty year investment performance. If there is no correlation, repeat the study and look at the 10 year investment performance. If no correlation, look at 5 years, etc.

If you do not find correlation between volatility and performance for the longer term periods, see if you can find a short term in which there is a correlation. If there is a correlation in the short term, at what length of time does that correlation disappear? Is there any correlation even for a very short term? I expect that the correlation between day to day volatility and investment performance, if it exists, is a short term phenomenon.

**If the correlation between day to day volatility and investment performance is only a short term phenomenon, then the use of the day to day volatility as a measure of risk is useless and/or harmful in decision making for long term investing.**

What have others said about these issues?

Mark Hulbert, a journalist for Market Watch began an article in the Wall Street Journal (October 5, 2020, page R3) with the following sentence: "A bedrock principle of investment theory is that over time, the high risk/reward shares known as high-beta stocks will make more money than low-beta stocks." In the chapter above, I have argued against the truth of that "bedrock principle" when investing for the long term.

Mark Hulbert is quoted in Wikipedia (October 6, 2020) as stating, "Simply put, the odds are overwhelming that ---over the long term ---- you will make more money by buying and holding an index fund." Wikipedia further quotes Mark Hulbert as saying that **real investors are** "…**unable to hold an index fund through a bear market, and by selling near the bottom they fail to realize** ….[the] **theoretical long term potential."** (bolding mine)

In the Scientific American (March 2011, Page 77) Michael Shermer writes "Stossel cited a study in the journal Economics and Portfolio Strategy that tracked 452 managed funds from 1990 to 2009, finding that only 13 beat the market average. Equating managed fund directors to 'snake-oil salesmen,' Malkiel said that Wall Street is selling Main Street on the belief that experts can consistently time the market and make accurate predictions of when to buy and sell. They can't. No one can."

From the website of the Institute for Pension Fund Integrity (Dated August 2019, seen on October 10, 2020) there is a "Report on Public Pension Performance: Comparing Pension Investments to Passive Index Portfolios." The Overview section begins "While the stock market has boomed since the Great Recession, public pension plans remain woefully underfunded and underperforming." The report goes on to say: "In an effort to provide another tool to our retired and retiring public employees and teachers, to understand the health of their state pension plans, we created two passive index investment portfolios comprised of 50% stocks and 50% bonds, and 60% stocks and 40% bonds. We then compared each state's pension fund investment performance on an annualized ten-year basis to the performance of the index portfolio. This shows the relative performance per state, allowing for comparison of a state's pension performance across the country. Our full methodology is detailed below. What our analysis found was that the majority of the pension funds did not outperform both the 60/40, and 50/50 stocks and bonds passive index portfolios, and that those states that allow politics to influence their investment strategy more than other states generally performed worse."

Note please the emphasis on comparing pension fund performance to portfolios of 50% to 60% stocks and 40% to 50% bonds. These percentages come right from the" efficient frontier" of the Modern Portfolio Theory. Why are the pension funds doing so poorly? Poor management. High costs. Political interference. Excessive diversification to minimize short term volatility. You can do better than any of these massive pension funds!

"What made these economists love the efficient-market theory was that the math was so elegant, and after all, the math was what they had learned to do. To a man with a hammer, every problem seems to pretty much look like a nail. The alternative truth was a little messy, and they'd forgotten the great economist Keynes, who I think said, "**Better to be roughly right than precisely wrong**."" (Charlie Munger, 1995, Speech at Harvard University) (bolding mine)

From the Marketwatch website, October 10, 2020, an article by Mark Hulbert titled, "What the Harvard endowment's below-average grade can teach you about index funds and your investments." Included in the article: "Harvard's University's endowment's return lagged the U.S. stock market — again." …. "This marks the 12th year in a row in which the $42 billion portfolio fell behind the benchmark index." He continues: "It would be easy to smugly write off Harvard's performance as the comeuppance due to a bunch of elites who think they are smarter than the rest of us. But that would be a mistake, since by doing that we would miss important investment lessons that can be drawn from Harvard's experience."

He then emphasizes "Performance persistence is rare," "Overconfidence is an obstacle," and "Reversion to the mean is a powerful force," He then states "It is almost impossible, over not just the short term but also over the intermediate term, to know whether performance is due to luck or skill." He points out that "Over the past 20 years, for example, Harvard's endowment has lagged a portfolio that invested 60% in an S&P 500 index fund and 40% in a U.S. bond market index fund (4.8% annualized versus 5.8%, according to my calculations)." He continues "Index-fund pioneer John Bogle was right: Given that index funds are so difficult to beat, it's hard to justify paying the salaries of a large high-priced staff to run the endowment." He ends his article with this quote "The bottom line? Beating the stock market is incredibly difficult. Over the past 20 years you could have beaten Harvard's endowment by putting your money in index funds and doing nothing else. That's amazing to contemplate. What other pursuit in life is there in which you can do better than the best and the brightest by doing nothing?" The behavior of Harvard in persisting with their poorly performing investment program is the "escalation of commitment" behavior, I discussed in the chapter on the psychology of investment.

From the Marketwatch Website; October 25, 2020; an article by Michael Edesess: Headline: "Why those highly paid investing pros do worse than a 401(k) committed to a boring stock index fund". Sub-headline: "High fees take a toll on performance, no matter how bright and brilliant you are". Edesess references a report in the Journal of Portfolio Management by Richard M. Ennis. The article states: "The educational endowments of top universities including Harvard, Yale, Princeton and Stanford are gigantic pools of money …. They are managed by highly qualified and well-paid experts who have access to professors in the finance departments at their universities ….. Wouldn't you think that these funds would achieve better investment results than, say, a middle-class worker whose money is invested in her 401(k)'s low-cost index fund …. But they don't. In fact ….. they achieve worse results. …. Their shortfall in performance is almost exactly equal to the excess fees they pay. ….. According to Ennis, **large endowments pay on average a steep 1.6% annual fee -- exactly the amount by which they underperform the middle-class investors 401(k) index fund.**" (bolding mine)

Edesess continues, "The trouble is, because ordinary investors don't understand that it is all for show and no actual use at all, they are inveigled by snow jobs sold to them by purveyors of investment schemes that are meant to make ordinary investors believe they are 'sophisticated,' and therefore will do better." Edesess finishes his report with this, "It can be a mistake to put too much faith in expertise. In the investment management field, this truth is spectacularly apparent."

Regarding my argument that the stock market is less efficient than the bond market, Steve Keen, in "Debunking Economics", 2nd edition, 2011, page 22, refers to "… the fallacies that finance markets always price financial assets correctly …" Steve Keen is currently professor and head of the School of Economic, History and Politics at Kingston University in London. (Wikipedia, November 13, 2020)

Regarding my comments about investor behavior causing the increased volatility in the stock market, Keen mentions Keynes when stating "Expectations are therefore bound to be fragile, since future circumstances almost inevitably turn out to be different from what we expected. This volatility in expectations will mean sudden shifts in investor (and speculator) sentiment, which will suddenly change the values placed on assets, to the detriment of anyone whose assets are held in non-liquid form." (Keen, page 227)

Regarding my critique of the Modern Portfolio Theory, here are some other quotes from Steve Keen, "Debunking Economics", 2nd edition, 2011.

"Theories can therefore be evaluated by their assumptions to some extent, if one has an intelligent taxonomy of assumptions. … But it will be hobbled if those assumptions specify the domain of the theory, and real-world phenomena are outside the domain." (Keen, pages 163)

"Assumptions matter in a more profound sense because, as this book shows, assumptions can be logically incoherent. ….. A theory that contains logically inconsistent assumptions will be a bad theory – and, as this book shows, economics is replete with logical inconsistencies" (Keen, page 164)

"The core beliefs are known as the 'hard core' – since they cannot be altered without rejecting, in some crucial sense, the very foundations of the science." (Keen, page 165)

Note: In the quotes below Keen uses the words risk and uncertainty differently than I do and differently than common usage. He uses risk to describe the situation in which there is sufficient data to perform a calculation of the statistical probability of something happening. He uses uncertainty to describe the situation in which there is insufficient data to determine the statistical probability of something happening.

"Risk applies to situations in which the regularity of past events is a reliable guide to the course of future events." … "A risky event will have a probability associated with it, and a variance of outcomes around those probabilities, which can be reliably estimated using the techniques of statistics. Uncertainty applies when the past provides no reliable guide to future events. Though the fact that we cannot predict the future is the essence of the human condition, the very nebulousness of uncertainty means that many people – and certainly the vast majority of economists – have difficulty grasping the concept. **As a result, they act as if the quantifiable concept of risk can be safely substituted for unquantifiable uncertainty**." (Keen, page 161) (bolding mine) I argue that Modern Portfolio Theory does exactly what is stated in the quote above.

**I argue that Modern Portfolio Theory uses the quantifiable standard deviation of the day to day volatility of any basket of assets to estimate risk in the real life situation of unquantifiable uncertainty for the long term future.**

And another Keen quote: "**Past trends therefore cannot be confidently extrapolated to predict future performance – but this procedure is the essential assumption behind using statistics to calculate risk.**" ….. "**The assumption that risk can be used as a proxy for uncertainty when evaluating investments is therefore unrealistic.** A theory that makes such an assumption is quite clearly not better than an alternative one which does not – quite the opposite in fact." (Keen, page 162) (bolding mine) I argue that Modern Portfolio Theory makes the incorrect assumption that risk (Keen's definition of risk) can be used as a proxy for real life uncertainty (Keen's definition of uncertainty).

"Uncertainty introduces an asymmetry into people's reactions to losses and gains, and this results in a multitude of ways in which people's behavior deviates from the predictions of the Efficient Market Hypothesis". … "Many of these behaviors are also clearly counterproductive in the context of stock market gambling, and in turn they make it highly likely that market prices will deviate substantially from 'innate value.'" (Keen, page 384) Hence, the greater volatility of the stock market.

"Haugen presents the alternative case for 'a noisy stock market that over-reacts to past records of success and failure on the part of business firms, and prices with great imprecision." (Keen, page 389)

"In fact, in today's stock market, the major news will always be the most recent movements in stock prices, rather than 'real' news from the economy." (Keen, page 389)

"Haugen argues that there are three sources of volatility: event-driven, error-driven, and price driven" … "The third is the phenomenon of the market reacting to its own volatility, building price movements upon price movements, in the same way that neighborhood dogs can sometimes keep yelping almost indefinitely after one of them has started." (Keen, page 389)

Some quotes from John Maynard Keynes (The General Theory of Employment, Interest and Money, 1936, Chapter 12): John Maynard Keynes "was a British economist, whose ideas fundamentally changed the theory and practice of macroeconomics and the economic policies of governments." (Wikipedia, November 13, 2020)

"If we speak frankly, we have to admit that our basis of knowledge for estimating the yield ten years hence of a railway, a copper mine, a textile factory, the goodwill of a patent medicine, an Atlantic liner, a building in the City of London amounts to little and sometimes to nothing; or even five years hence." (Keynes, Chapter 12, III) **This is consistent with the fact that the day to day volatility of an investment in any of these assets has no bearing on its value in five to ten years.**

"Day-to-day fluctuations in the profits of existing investments, which are obviously of an ephemeral and non-significant character, tend to have an altogether excessive, and even an absurd, influence on the market." (Keynes, Chapter 12, V)

"Finally it is the long-term investor, he who most promotes the public interest, who will in practice come in for most criticism, wherever investment funds are managed by committees or boards or banks. For it is in the essence of his behaviour that he should be eccentric, unconventional and rash in the eyes of average opinion. If he is successful, that will only confirm the general belief in his rashness; and if in the short run he is unsuccessful, which is very likely, he will not receive much mercy. **Worldly wisdom teaches that it is better for reputation to fail conventionally than to succeed unconventionally.**" (Keynes, Chapter 12, V) (bolding mine)

"A conventional valuation which is established as the outcome of the mass psychology of a large number of ignorant individuals is liable to change violently as the result of a sudden fluctuation of opinion due to factors which do not really make much difference to the prospective yield…In abnormal times in particular…the market will be subject to waves of optimistic and pessimistic sentiment, which are unreasoning and yet in a sense legitimate where no solid basis exists for a reasonable calculation." (Keynes, Chapter 12, V)

"For most of these persons are, in fact, largely concerned…with foreseeing changes in the conventional basis of valuation a short time ahead of the general public. They are concerned, not with what an investment is really worth to a man who buys it "for keeps", but with what the market will value it at, under the influence of mass psychology, three months or a year hence". (Keynes, Chapter 12, V)

"life is not long enough; — human nature desires quick results, there is a peculiar zest in making money quickly, and remoter gains are discounted by the average man at a very high rate." (Keynes, Chapter 12, V)

Regarding my opinions regarding the under pricing of bonds, refer to the Wall Street Journal, November 17, 2020 in the section labelled "Heard on the Street: Financial Analysis and Commentary, Page B11: there is an article titled "Yields of 0.9% Have Appeal." Within the article it states: "**getting paid 0.9% annually to lock money away for 10 years has rarely looked more tempting.**" Later in the article: "For an ultra safe asset in 2020, though this may be a window of opportunity." Regarding expecting short term trends to remain long term: "Inflation hasn't reached uncomfortable levels for decades, so investors have become convinced that rates will be stuck at zero even after the economy recovers from Covid-19." And: "This year, fear has pushed the term premium further into negative territory." And: "Markets may be riding a new wave of optimism, but investors still need a hedge against the massive uncertainties of the months ahead." And finally: "**In a world of rates stuck at zero, a risk-free asset that yields 0.9% should be quite appealing.**" (bolding mine) Need I say more about the under pricing of bonds and the false sense of the safety of bonds when investing for ten, twenty or more years. This article is all about short term safety; note the comments: "getting paid 0.9%

annually to lock money away for 10 years has rarely looked more tempting" and "ultra safe asset in 2020" and "investors still need a hedge against the massive uncertainties of the months ahead." Nowhere is there any sense of investing with a time horizon of ten, twenty or more years.

To summarize my "Critique of Modern Portfolio Theory":

1. All theories start with one or more assumptions. Rene Descartes began with "Cogito, ergo sum." As of this moment, I believe, this beginning assumption has not been disproved.
2. If you start a theory with a false assumption, no amount of mathematics will make that theory correct.
3. Modern Portfolio Theory starts with the assumption that the day to day volatility of a basket of assets is a valid measure of the risk of investing in that basket of assets for any time horizon.
4. All of the conclusions that flow from the mathematics of Modern Portfolio Theory depend for their veracity on the truth of Modern Portfolio Theory's assumption of how to measure the risk of investing in a basket of assets.
5. I have argued that the assumption that the day to day volatility of a basket of assets is a valid measure of the risk of investing in a basket of assets is incorrect particularly for long term horizons. I have argued that the day to day volatility is a short term phenomenon that does not offer useful information for investing with a long term horizon.
6. I have argued that the reason that stocks perform better than bonds over the long term is that for a long time bonds have been considered so safe that much of the financial world is willing to buy bonds for less than they should be worth. Stated another way, investors are willing to buy bonds for much lower interest rates than they should. Stated another way, purchasers of bonds have been willing to accept the poor long term investment performance of bonds for the illusion of safety. Stated another way, bonds have been under priced for a long time.

7. I have argued that the fact that stocks have higher volatility than bonds is due to the differential "efficiency" in determining the value of each type of investment which, in turn, changes investor behavior.
8. I have argued that the excessive diversification which results from attempting to minimize day to day volatility leads to lower long term investment results due to investing in lower performing assets.
9. I argue that the unnecessary complexity which results from following the Modern Portfolio Theory leads to the costly use of financial managers which harms long term investing results.
10. One final thought: If the financial world listens to me and the investing results from bonds and stocks equalize, then much of what I have written will no longer be valid.

# CHAPTER TEN:
# Diversification

I have already addressed the subject of diversification in my chapter critiquing Modern Portfolio Theory. I wish to continue my discussion of diversification as a separate topic.

Definition:
"In finance, diversification is the process of allocating capital in a way that reduces exposure to any one particular asset or risk. A common path towards diversification is to reduce risk or volatility by investing in a variety of assets. If asset prices do not change in perfect synchrony, a diversified portfolio will have less variance than the weighted average variance of its constituent assets and often less volatility than the least volatile of its constituents." (Wikipedia, September 10, 2020)

My, how the math creeps in. Note, the use of the phrase "weighted average variance." Suddenly, you think, I can't do this. Why? Because it seems so complicated! I will keep it simple.

Note this partial quote from the definition above:

**"In finance, diversification is the process of allocating capital in a way that reduces exposure to any one particular asset or risk."**

This is true! This makes sense! This is simple! This works! So, how should you diversify? How much should you diversify? It seems obvious to me and I assume that it is obvious to you that it is not smart to put all of your money into one stock. Remember the old saying, "Don't put all of your eggs in one basket."

Why?

If that one company, whose stock you own, goes bankrupt, you have lost everything. Yes, that one stock may skyrocket up, but the risk of losing everything is too great. So, how many different assets provides sufficient diversification?

Here is where much of the discussion regarding how much diversification is proper leans on Modern Portfolio Theory and its emphasis on the day to day volatility of your basket of assets as the accepted measure of risk.

The Wikipedia definition of diversification above also included this partial quote: "A common path towards diversification is to reduce risk or volatility by investing in a variety of assets." This part of the Wikipedia definition of diversification suggests that part of the purpose of diversification is to minimize the day to day volatility definition of risk seen in the Modern Portfolio Theory.

Let's look at diversification from the Modern Portfolio Theory point of view. One stock has its own day to day volatility. To a certain extent, there will be seemingly random daily ups and downs in the value of that stock. If we add a second stock and put equal money in each stock, there will be some days one of the two stocks goes up while the other goes down in value and vice versa. Thus, the overall volatility of two stocks will on average be less than either single stock. Similarly, a portfolio of three stocks will have less volatility than a portfolio of two stocks. The combined volatility is less if the stocks are in different industries. At somewhere between ten and thirty stocks the decrease in day to day volatility of the combined portfolio ceases to decrease significantly with the addition of yet another stock to the portfolio.

From Wikipedia (September 30, 2020) "There is no magic number of stocks that is diversified versus not. Sometimes quoted is 30, although it can be as low as 10, provided they are carefully chosen. This is based on a result from John Evans and Stephen Archer. Similarly, a 1985 book reported that most of the value from diversification comes from the first 15 or 20 different stocks in a portfolio."

So, if you are going to follow Modern Portfolio Theory, somewhere between 15 and 30 different stocks satisfies the mathematical statistical concerns regarding lowering the day to day volatility of your basket of assets. Should you follow these statistical results? Are these statistical results sensible?

If you are going to choose a relatively small number of stocks for your investment portfolio, how are you to choose those stocks? As mentioned before, there are many others out there with more training and more time than you. Really, how can you reasonably expect to out choose them? Without belaboring the issue of exactly how many stocks are sufficient, it is clear that choosing a much larger number of stocks will prevent you from making a few seriously wrong choices of which stocks to buy. Low cost stock index mutual funds or ETFs solve that problem for you easily and cheaply.

I repeat: Statistically, most of the benefit from diversification is reached after adding approximately twenty assets to your basket of assets. Statistics are nice, BUT, if you are going to play games and try to choose the fewest assets possible, this means you are actively choosing these twenty stocks. Questions arise! Are you covering all of the different industry sectors properly? Why do you think you are good enough to personally choose those twenty stocks.

While twenty stocks may make the statisticians happy, it will not protect you from picking stocks poorly. Sticking with low cost all stock index funds fully satisfies diversification while avoiding diversifying into low performing assets just to lower day to day volatility.

There are others who recommend and practice more extensive diversification. My discussion of CalPERS in the previous chapter was an example of extensive diversification. Maximum diversification is also known as a "buying the market portfolio." Identifying the "buying the market portfolio" is not straightforward. One definition comes from the capital asset pricing model which argues the maximum diversification comes from buying a pro rata share of all available assets. At the extreme, diversification has no maximum so long as more assets are available. Every equally weighted, uncorrelated asset can be added to a portfolio and increase that portfolio's measured diversification. When assets are not uniformly uncorrelated, a weighting approach that puts assets in proportion to their relative correlation can maximize the available diversification.

The capital asset pricing model was mentioned above.

Definition:
"In finance, the capital asset pricing model (CAPM) is a model used to determine a theoretically appropriate required rate of return of an asset, to make decisions about adding assets to a well-diversified portfolio. " … "The model takes into account the asset's sensitivity to non-diversifiable risk (also known as systemic risk or market risk), often represented by the quantity Beta ($\beta$) in the financial industry, as well as the expected return of the market and the expected return of a theoretical free risk asset. (Wikipedia, October 3, 2020)

I do not expect you to understand the definition above. I am not sure that I do. I include it to provide some flavor for the theoretical mathematical hoops the "so called experts" generate. This is the background for the decisions the "so called experts" are making when they recommend maximum diversification. This is the theoretical background where the basic assumption of Modern Portfolio Theory that the actual risk of investing in your basket of assets is defined by the day to day volatility of the value of your basket of assets is taken to its extreme. This is the theoretical background that leads to the excessive diversification which, as I have noted before, places investment dollars in lower performing asset categories.

One point to remember about diversification. The total return of a diversified portfolio, by definition, will always be less than the best performing asset in the basket of assets. Likewise, the total return of a diversified portfolio will always be better than the worst performing asset in that basket of assets. Thus, you will never do as well as the best performing asset and never do as poorly as the worst performing asset. This is a good thing! It is what you expect from diversification.

Steel yourself against the hindsight "regret" of thinking, "I should have put all of my money into the best performing asset." You can never know ahead of time which asset will turn out to be the best performing asset. You will always know "in hindsight" which was the best performing asset.

Let me return to the basic question of this chapter. What is the purpose of diversification? Is the purpose of diversification to minimize the day to day volatility of your basket of assets or is the purpose of diversification to minimize the risk of significant loss due to serious long term underperformance of one or a few assets? As discussed in the previous chapter, I believe that following Modern Portfolio Theory results in excessive diversification which leads to underperformance with respect to investing with long time horizons. I am not against diversification. I am in favor of diversification, just not to an excessive degree.

Your financial advisors and financial managers will show you colorful images indicating the eight or ten or twelve different categories of assets you should be invested in to be fully diversified. Sometimes more than eight or ten. The financial advisors and financial managers make investing seem so complex, that you lose confidence and say to yourself "I can never do this."

I repeat:

Extensive diversification into multiple types of assets clearly lowers the day to day volatility of your basket of assets, which is the gold standard of the Modern Portfolio Theory. But, this extensive diversification diversifies you into lower performing assets all in the name of lowering the day to day volatility of the total value of your basket of assets.

As I have stated before, I think diversification through low cost index stock mutual funds is the ideal. This is contrary to what most financial advisors and managers will recommend. Another reason your advisors and managers don't like low cost index funds; they don't provide much profit for the advisors, the managers or the financial firm.

For the past one hundred years or more United States stocks have performed better over any twenty year time horizon than any complicated mixture of assets. For almost all ten year time horizons United States stocks have outperformed complicated diversified portfolios. For the few they did not, it was only by a small percentage.

There are numerous low cost United States stock index funds available to invest in. Some diversification into growth and value stocks and into small cap, mid cap and large cap stocks makes sense.

In summary:

Diversify but don't overdo it. Everything in moderation! So where and how should you diversify? Following the mandate of Modern Portfolio Theory to minimize day to day volatility leads to excessive diversification. Excessive diversification leads to investing in low performing assets which lowers long term horizon investment performance.

My concerns that bonds are currently under priced and have been for over a century leads me to recommend against using bonds to diversify. Using bonds to diversify leads to investing in a low performing class of assets for a long term investing horizon. While this may change in the future, bonds have underperformed stocks historically for any twenty year investment time horizon in the past.

Diversifying into international stocks seems like a good idea. Recognize that whatever percentage you choose to place in international stocks will be purely arbitrary. My concern with diversifying into international stocks includes the involvement of autocratic countries in most of the international stock mutual funds and ETFs. My concerns also involve my self awareness that I am unable to judge the stability of international countries and their economies. I am also unable to judge the relative stabilities of international currencies. International investment seems less transparent to me.

Following the statisticians and investing in as few as thirty stocks risks making poor choices regarding which stocks to buy. So, I end up diversifying mainly with United States stocks in low cost stock index funds. This makes it easy to diversify in terms of number of stocks and easy to keep the yearly cost of investing low. In terms of transparency, I recognize that I end up betting on the health of the United States economy going forward. I recognize that nothing lasts forever and that I will need to constantly re-evaluate this decision.

# CHAPTER ELEVEN:
# Rebalancing

I previously mentioned the issue of rebalancing when discussing the investing results of CalPERS in my chapter critiquing Modern Portfolio Theory. I wish to discuss rebalancing as a separate topic.

Definition:
"The rebalancing of investments (or Constant Mix) is the action / trading strategy of bringing a portfolio that has deviated away from one's target asset allocation back into line. This can be implemented by transferring assets, that is, selling investments in an asset class that is overweight and using the money to buy investments in a class that is underweight, but it also applies to adding or removing money from a portfolio, that is, putting new money into an underweight class, or making withdrawals from an overweight class." (Wikipedia, September 11, 2020)

Financial advisors and managers often spend a great deal of time discussing and recommending rebalancing of your portfolio. This advice is often given for rebalancing the relative fraction of stocks versus bonds, the relative fraction of international stocks versus domestic stocks, the relative fraction of small capitalization stocks versus large capitalization stocks, etc.

What follows are some of my objections to rebalancing.

First.
Recognize that the choices of the comparative fractions of the assets (stocks vs bonds; domestic vs international; small cap vs large cap; growth vs. value, etc.) are truly arbitrary. Recall that the common choice of say 60% stocks and 40% bonds comes from the Modern Portfolio Theory's use of the efficient frontier in an attempt to minimize the day to day volatility of your basket of assets. I have argued previously that the day to day volatility of your basket of assets is a short term phenomenon which has no correlation with a long term buy and hold stock index mutual fund investing strategy. I have argued previously that the day to day volatility should be ignored. I have argued previously that investment decisions which arise from the use of the day to day volatility as a measure of risk should be ignored.

From my point of view, therefore, the 60/40 allocation of stocks and bonds is arbitrary. There is no reasonable theory which informs us concerning what relative fraction of stocks should be international stocks versus domestic stocks. Investments in international stocks involve more complex issues including questions of the stability of other countries, shifts in the value of international currencies and less transparency regarding what you are buying.

I am not specifically against investments in international assets. I know that I do not have sufficient knowledge to evaluate the stability of international countries. I know that I do not have the knowledge to judge the possibility of future fluctuations in international currencies. There is less transparency regarding international companies available to the average individual investor. It is harder to know specifically what you are investing in.

For example, a few years ago I was surprised to find that most emerging market mutual funds were more than 20% invested in mainland China assets. Prior to my discovering this, I was not aware that an emerging market mutual fund, I was invested in, had such a large investment in China assets. Upon discovering that, I transferred my funds out of that emerging market mutual fund. I did not reinvest in another emerging market mutual fund because I could not find an emerging market fund which avoided autocratic countries. My long term horizon risk concerns include possible political and economic instability in autocratic countries for the extended indeterminate future.

Also, whatever relative fractions of domestic and international assets you think are reasonable today, this may change depending on changes in the domestic and international environment. Currently in 2020, the United States seems the most stable country politically (despite the current political unrest) when compared with the rest of the world. Obviously, that could change quickly.

My point is that any stated comparative fractions of diverse assets are arbitrary. If you practice rebalancing, understand and admit to yourself that you are rebalancing to arbitrarily predetermined fractions of assets.

Then, ask yourself: Why? Why am I rebalancing to some arbitrarily predetermined fractionation of assets? How do you know that your arbitrary fractionation of assets is best? You don't know. You can't know. The answer is unknowable.

Second:
Another issue I have with rebalancing is this.

Let's assume you have two investments, A and B, and you decide that you want each investment to account for 50% of your portfolio. One investment, A, increases on average at the rate of 10% per year and the other, B, increases on average at the rate of 2% per year. If you rebalance each year, then each year you will transfer money from the A investment to the B investment. This will result in a significantly lower long term investment result than if you did not rebalance. In this example, you are repetitively transferring money from a higher earning asset into a lower earning asset.

Obviously, this is a simplified example, but it serves to illustrate one of the potential problems with automatic rebalancing. The risk of repetitively transferring money from better performing investments to lower performing investments.

Here is a contrary example.

If there were two investments which oscillated such that one always went up when the other went down and vice versa, then rebalancing at carefully selected time intervals would increase the resultant investment returns. Simply put, the world doesn't work that way. No investments reliably behave that way.

Third.
If you are selling assets and buying other assets in order to rebalance, you may be selling the better performing assets having made a profit. You will have to pay capital gains taxes on the assets you sell. The rate of capital gains tax has varied over the years. Whatever it is, you are investing less money in the lower performing asset than you took out of the better performing asset. Current long term capital gains tax in the United States is 0%, 15% or 20% depending on your income. If you sell assets to rebalance and pay 15% capital gains tax on $100 capital gains, you then have $85 dollars to invest. Your new rebalanced investment has to increase by 17.65% just to break even (15/85=0.1765) on the capital gains profit. Paying tax now rather than paying tax later harms your long term investing goals. This third argument does not pertain to investments in IRAs or 401ks under current law.

Reprise:
In summary, if you rebalance, you are rebalancing to arbitrarily predetermined fractions of your portfolio. Look in the mirror and admit that these predetermined fractions are arbitrary. If you admit that these fractions are arbitrary, then recognize the folly of trying to rebalance to fractions which are arbitrary. Another point: Rebalancing takes money from the better perform-

ing part of your portfolio and transfers it to the lower performing part of your portfolio and this makes sense because ……? I can't answer that question. I don't think it makes sense. Finally, rebalancing has tax consequences as well.

What have others said?

In the Wall Street Journal (January 9, 2017, Page R4), Robert Powell writes: "To many it is an unassailable principle: Investors should periodically rebalance their portfolios to their target mix of stocks, bonds, cash and alternatives that best suits their risk tolerance. Doing so is widely considered a best practice for reaching one's long-term financial goals." Later in the article he writes: "If their (two or more types of assets) performance diverges by more than a small amount, …. Then buy-and-hold will greatly outperform rebalancing." Later in the article: "…rebalancing makes two false assumptions: One, that all securities are cyclical and regress to a mean … and two, that all regressions to the mean take the same amount of time."

# CHAPTER TWELVE:
# Borrowing

What is borrowing?

Simply put in financial terms, if I borrow money from you, you allow me to use some of your money for a period of time. You loan me some money. What do I have to do to get you to loan me money? If you are not my friend giving me a free loan, I have to pay you interest on the money you loan me. I have to give you more money back, than you gave me in the first place.

Who wins? Often both parties win. The entity loaning the money wins because the lender ends up with more money after the loan and interest are paid back. The borrower wins if the money is invested and used to make more money. The borrower wins if the money is used for a worthwhile purpose, such as buying a house or a car. Otherwise, only in times of high inflation might the borrower "win", because the borrower pays the loan back with money that is worth less than it was when the loan occurred.

Why should anyone ever borrow money?

When you need the money for something important!

When you know you can afford to pay back the loan and the extra money owed as interest!

For anything that is not important:

**IF YOU CAN'T AFFORD IT NOW, YOU CAN'T AFFORD IT. PERIOD!**

Let me repeat.

For anything that is not important:

**IF YOU CAN'T AFFORD IT NOW, YOU CAN'T AFFORD IT. PERIOD!**

You only borrow for something really important.

Borrowing money is one of the easiest and surest ways to get into serious financial trouble.

If you don't pay off your credit card each month you are borrowing money. You are not only borrowing money you are borrowing money at exorbitantly high interest rates.

If you don't have enough money to buy something now, what makes you think you will have that money later?

When you pay a debt back, you pay with after tax dollars. Let's say you are in a 20% tax bracket. For every five dollars you earn, you pay one dollar to the IRS and four to pay off your loan. In addition, you are accruing interest all the while.

When should you borrow money?

To buy a house, yes, BUT: I repeat, BUT: I repeat BUT, can you really afford the house. If you can afford to buy a house, it is a great investment. The ideal is to pay off your mortgage. Do not use the value of your house as a bank from which to borrow money for things you don't need.

**ONCE YOU HAVE PAID OFF YOUR HOUSE MORTGAGE, YOU ARE THEN ABLE TO LIVE RENT FREE FOR THE REST OF YOUR LIFE!**

I repeat:

**ONCE YOU HAVE PAID OFF YOUR HOUSE MORTGAGE, YOU ARE THEN ABLE TO LIVE RENT FREE FOR THE REST OF YOUR LIFE!**

Do not think of your house as a bank you can borrow from. If you do, when are you ever going to pay your mortgage off? If you still owe money on a mortgage when you retire and your income drops drastically, where is the money going to come from to finish paying off your mortgage?

For most of us, it is necessary to borrow money to buy a car. Let me discuss the difference between leasing a car and buying one. If you lease a car you pay a lot of money for a few year's use of the car. Then you return the car and own nothing. Car leases often have limits to the mileage you can put on the car. If you go over the mileage limit, it is expensive. Automobile dealers like to lease you a car. Why? When the lease is over, you have to lease or buy another car.

If you buy a car you do not have a time limit or a mileage limit. You can keep your car for ten years or more. Once the car is paid off, it is a lot cheaper to run. Next, what car should you buy? If money is an issue look for an inexpensive car with a good general repair record in Consumer Reports or similar organization. Do you really need that expensive car? Can you really afford that expensive car? Will buying that expensive car really make you happier?

Often, it is effective to play games with ourselves.

Here is a recommendation for buying a car. Let's say you buy a reasonable car and borrow money to pay it off in three to five years.

After you finish paying off the car, continue to make your car payments.

What? What do I mean by this?

You have budgeted money to pay off the car. Once the car is paid off, continue making your car payments, but deposit these payments into a separate "car" bank account. If you keep your car for ten years, you will then have enough money in the "car" bank account to pay cash for your next car.

This way you cease borrowing from other people.

This way you cease paying interest to other people.

This way you are getting ahead of the game.

When borrowing I always try to avoid paying points. Points are fees paid up front to get the lender to lend you the money. Houses are often sold after a few years due to life and job changes. Paying points results in the loan costing you more. I personally consider points a legal "bribe" to convince the lender to loan me the money. I am willing to pay a higher interest rate than pay points. With inflation, the interest I pay later is worth less than the money I pay now in points.

Some NEVERS.:

NEVER! NEVER! NEVER!

Borrow money for a vacation, for a honeymoon, for a diamond ring, for fancy furniture. If you don't have the money for these now, you can't afford them. If you borrow for education, be careful how much you borrow. You run the risk of becoming an indentured servant never being able to pay off a large loan. Better to go to a community college and work and pay as you go. Never borrow for an airplane or yacht unless you have more money than you know what to do with. Do you really need it now? Do you really need that expensive fancy car? Are you saving enough for your retirement? Are you investing wisely in anticipation of retirement?

Consider your level of spending. Use self-discipline in deciding what to buy and what to spend.

I am not a fan of signing contracts in which I promise to pay money for a year or two to some entity. A gym membership is a perfect example of this. I belong to my local YMCA. The YMCA does not require a membership contract. You pay by the month. You start when you wish. You stop when you wish. If you lose your job, you are not stuck with a contract you cannot afford. In essence a gym contract is the same as borrowing money and promising to pay it back over time. Do you really need that fancy gym?

Do not borrow money for fancy furniture. Simple, used furniture works just fine. When my wife and I got married, we bought a used dining room table and six chairs from the Dover Country Store in Dover, Massachusetts for $50. We used the furniture for five years and sold it back to Dover Country Store for $55. There was double-digit inflation during those five years which explains why we seemed to get more money back from selling the furniture back to the store. The dollars were not worth as much.

Do not borrow money for Christmas gifts. If you cannot afford to pay for the Christmas gifts now, what makes you think you will be able to afford them in three months? If you cannot afford to pay for the Christmas gifts now, you cannot afford the Christmas gifts now. There is the old saying, "It is the thought that counts." Stop a moment and ask yourself why you have to spend so much money on Christmas presents anyway. Moderate your spending.

Credit cards. First, "Know thyself." Short of a true family financial emergency, you should be paying off your credit cards every month. The interest rate charged on many credit cards is astronomical. True usury. When I say know thyself, what I mean is, if you are unable to control your personal spending, destroy your credit card. This is part of playing games with yourself. A debit card, at least, limits your spending to whatever is in your bank account.

I want to discuss **the difference between long term debt and short term debt.**

In corporate finance there is extensive discussion between the advantages and disadvantages of long term debt vs short term debt. Short term debt is cheaper than long term debt. That is, the interest rate is lower for short term debt than long term debt. Due to the uncertainty regarding the future of inflation and interest rates, lenders require you to pay more to borrow for a long time, such as a fifteen or thirty year fixed mortgage.

For a home mortgage, an adjustable rate mortgage (ARM) is cheaper initially than a fixed rate mortgage of fifteen or thirty years. From the bank's point of view, **an ARM is short term debt.** The mortgage rate may be adjusted by the lender after one, three or five years or other time period depending on the ARM contract. An ARM mortgage is "safer" for the lender because the lender can raise the interest rate if inflation occurs and interest rates rise.

Think about this!

**An ARM transfers risk from the bank to the borrower**.

You, the borrower, are taking a big risk, namely the risk that interest rates will rise quickly, your mortgage payments will rise quickly and you will not be able to afford the increased mortgage payments!

An ARM is "better" for the borrower short term because the interest rate is lower initially.

**An ARM is dangerous for the borrower long term.**

Unexpected inflation and an unexpected increase in general interest rates may lead to a rise in the ARM mortgage interest rate which the borrower does not expect. If you have an ARM and interest rates rise, you may be unable to afford your mortgage payments. You may lose your house and the money you have already paid in.

**I RECOMMEND AGAINST USING ADJUSTABLE RATE MORTGAGES!**

If you can't afford a fixed rate mortgage, you can't afford a mortgage. A fixed rate mortgage provides you the safety and security that you know what your monthly payments will be GUARANTEED for the next 15 or 30 years. Don't take the risk that interest rates will shoot up. Let the bank take that risk! With inflation, the money you are paying for that mortgage in twenty years is worth a lot less than when you took out the mortgage.

Take a 30-year fixed mortgage. Then pay it off. Do not borrow more on your house. Do not use your house as a bank. Get the house paid off and then live rent free for the rest of your life.

Back to long term and short term borrowing. Long term interest rates are higher. However, a long term loan can't be called. This means that the bank or lending institution cannot suddenly, out of the blue, call you to demand that you pay off your loan without warning.

If you borrow for a short period of time, at end of that short term you may not be able to refinance at all. In tight times, think of the 2008 financial crisis, you may not be able to refinance. In tight times, short term rates may go way up making a loan more expensive than you can afford. If rates go down in the short term you can always refinance a long term loan. If there is high inflation, with a long term loan, you end up paying back the loan with cheaper money.

I am going to discuss a concept called **net present value (NPV)**. It is not important that you understand it. It is certainly not important that you be able to calculate it. I am presenting it because I want you to understand one method financiers use to calculate the value of investments. I want you to understand why banks want you to pay points when you borrow money from them. I repeat: It is not important that you understand net present value calculations. However, I do want you to understand the concept of **the time value of money**.

Question:

Is $1000 today worth more, less or the same as $1000 ten years from now?

It seems obvious to me that $1000 is worth less in 10 years than it is now. I hope that it is obvious to you. Let's look at this question more closely. If I have $1000 today I can invest it in "safe" U.S. treasury notes or bank certificates of deposit (CDs) and earn money by investing the $1000 reasonably safely. Thus, in ten years I will have more than the $1000, I started with. That is one reason why $1000 today is worth more than $1000 ten years from now. I can invest it to gain more money. Another reason that $1000 today is worth more than $1000 in ten years is inflation. Continuing inflation steadily erodes the value of money. $1000 in ten years is worth less than $1000 now. In ten years, $1000 will be able to buy less than it is able to buy today.

Next question:

How much more is $1000 worth today than $1000 in ten years?

There are mathematical methods for trying to estimate the answer. I have promised no math. There will be no math. One method for trying to calculate an estimate for this difference in value is called a **net present value (NPV) calculation**. The details of how to calculate net present value (NPV) are available. They are studied in business school. I do not plan to discuss the mathematical details in this book.

In the discussion on inflation, I discussed how inflation erodes the value of money. The rule of 72 allowed for a rough, off the cuff determination of the rapidity of that erosion of value. Net Present Value calculations attempt greater precision in this estimate. NPV calculations allow for performing this type of calculation in situations involving complex cash flows.

Definition:
"In finance, the net present value (NPV) or net present worth (NPW) applies to a series of cash flows occurring at different times. The present value of a cash flow depends on the interval of time between now and the cash flow. It also depends on the discount rate. NPV accounts for the time value of money." (Wikipedia, September 30, 2020)

I repeat from the definition above:

"The present value of a cash flow depends on the interval of time between now and the cash flow."

"NPV accounts for the time value of money."

The definition of NPV mentioned that the NPV depends on the "discount rate."

What is the "discount rate?"

Definition:
"The discount rate is often the interest rate you can earn on your money." (Wikipedia, September 20, 2020) The "discount rate" chosen is the interest rate the person doing the calculation assumes is correct going forward into the future. The further into the future the calculation extends, the more arbitrary the "discount rate" chosen. It will be the rate the calculator assumes is correct extending into the future.

Let's look at a simple net present value calculation example.

Assume I invest $1000 now.

For investment A, I receive $300 a year for five years starting at the end of the first year. Thus, I receive a total of $1500 ($300 per year times five years) income by the end of the fifth year.

For investment B, I receive nothing for five years and then from years six through ten I receive $400 a year for five years. Thus, I receive a total of $2000 ($400 per year times five years) at the end of each year between years six and ten.

Which is the better investment?

Investment A pays $1500 and investment B pays $2000. Does this mean automatically that investment B is the better investment? Is $2000 paid between years 6 and 10 better or worse than $1500 paid between years 1 and 5? NPV calculations address this issue.

If the discount rate is low, for example 2%, then the NPV for investment A is $414 and for B is $708.

If the discount rate is high, for example 10%, then the NPV for investment A is $137 and for B is $58.

Let's compare the net present value results.

If inflation is low and interest rates are low, then the discount rate chosen will be low. In this example 2%. In that situation, investment B is considered superior. Compare $708 to $414. Money five to ten years in the future is still worth something. Money in the future is not discounted heavily at the low 2% discount rate. Thus, investment B is calculated to be worth more than investment A at the present time.

If inflation is high and interest rates are high, then the discount rate chosen will be high. In this example 10%. In that situation, investment A is considered superior. Compare $137 to $58. The income in the further future (years 6-10), even though greater in absolute number, is considered to be worth less at the present time. That is, the income in the further future is discounted to a greater extent. Thus, investment A is calculated to be worth more that investment B at the present time.

Note also, that the value for both investments is worth less in the present time in a high inflation, high interest rate (high discount rate) environment than in a low inflation, low interest rate (low discount rate) environment. For investment A compare $414 to $137 and for investment B compare $708 to $58. Note the greater difference occurred in the investment which paid out further into the future.

I repeat:

When inflation is high and interest rates are high, money in the future is calculated to be worth much less in a net present value calculation. The further into the future you go the more profound the influence of discounting on net present value. The time value of money changes with length of time into the future and with the interest rates.

If you did not understand my discussion of net present value, it is not important.

Simply put:

**Money in the future is worth less than money in the present.**

**In times of high inflation with corresponding high interest rates, money in the future is worth much, much less than money in the present.**

One last point, for anyone who actually uses NPV calculations in their work. Understand that the further into the future you extend your calculation, the less reliable it is.

Why?

You cannot accurately predict the inflation and interest rate environment in the future. Thus, an NPV calculation extended far into the future is nothing more than comforting, mental gymnastics.

Why did I detour into explaining net present value (NPV) calculations?

Why do banks and lending institutions want you to pay points when you take out a mortgage? Why do banks and financial institutions so often insist that you pay points to borrow money?

Two reasons.

One:
If you pay off your mortgage early, and many people do, then the banks have earned more money from your having paid points up front. People keep their houses on average between seven and twelve years. This depends on which years you examine. This also means that most 30 year mortgages are paid off in less than fifteen years. If you try to calculate the advantages and disadvantages of paying points on a 30 year mortgage, take into account the fact that it is unusual to stay in the same house for 30 years.

Two:
Money paid now is worth more than money paid later. (Recall my NPV discussion above) The banks really, really like for you pay more money now!

Points are often paid to obtain lower interest rates for home mortgages. I avoid points whenever possible. Rarely, a careful calculation may show that you benefit by paying points. Paying points is often negotiable. Remember:

The bank is not your friend. The bank wants to make as much money from you as it can.

The net present value discussion above demonstrates why the banks and lending institutions want you to pay points. The net present value discussion above demonstrates why you should avoid paying points if possible.

It is reasonable for a bank to make money from lending money to you. Otherwise, there would be no incentive to loan you money. Your job, when borrowing, is to obtain the best deal possible.

# CHAPTER THIRTEEN
# Choosing a financial advisor or financial manager ..... OR NOT!

Let's assume that I have not convinced you to take personal control of your finances and invest in a buy and hold long term low cost all United States stock mutual funds strategy.

Let's assume that you decide to choose a financial manager or financial advisor despite my advice.

How do you choose?

How do you find a "good" one?

How do you judge a prospective financial advisor or financial manager?

Great personality should be one of the least important categories to consider. Avoid gifts and attempts to manipulate you. Go back and read my chapter on psychology. I would avoid single person situations because of the higher risk of fraud. I would also avoid small firms with only a few principals for similar possible fraud concerns. Go back and read my chapter on "Who can you trust?" If you are subject to fraud and your advisor is part of a large financial firm, the large firm is more likely to make you "whole." Avoid sector rotation. That is, avoid investing in last year's number one ranked fund. For most number one ranked funds, the following year's performance is below average.

Do you pick a fund or an advisor or manager who has been successful over the past five or ten years?

Consider the following. This example is not original with me. I do not recall where I read it, so I am unable to offer proper citation. I am unable to find it with an internet search.

Assume you have 1024 armadillos who are trained to press either one of two levers for food. In the examples, I have read, authors use monkeys or human dart throwing. Using monkeys and darts seems trite, so I will go with armadillos. You use the random pushing of the levers for each of the 1024 armadillos to pick a portfolio of ten stocks to invest in for one year. Each year you have 1024 portfolios of ten randomly picked different stocks for each armadillo. Each year, each portfolio buys the ten stocks on January 1st and sells the ten stocks on December 31st. You then compare the investing results of all 1024 armadillos.

Fifty per cent of the armadillos or 512 armadillos will have investing results better than average for the first year. That results from simple random statistics. Similarly, fifty per cent or 512 armadillos will have investing results worse than average.

Repeat the same investing technique with the armadillos for a second year. By pure random statistical chance, 256 of the armadillos will have investing results better than average for two consecutive years. The half of the armadillos with better than average results the first year have a fifty per cent chance of being better than average the second year by pure random chance. Also, approximately 256 armadillos will be worse than average by pure random statistical chance two years in a row.

For the third year, 128 armadillos will have been better than average for three straight years from pure random chance by the same logic. For four years, 64 armadillos. For five years, 32 armadillos will have been better than average for five straight years from pure statistical chance. Also, 32 armadillos worse than average for five straight years from pure statistical chance.

For six years, 16 armadillos. For seven years, 8 armadillos. For eight years, 4 armadillos. For nine years, 2 armadillos. Finally, for ten years pure random statistical chance predicts that there will be one armadillo who has had investing results better than average every year for ten consecutive years. Also, for ten years pure random statistical chance predicts that there will probably be one armadillo (poor fellow) who has had investing results worse than average every year for ten consecutive years

Imagine that you do not know that armadillos are picking the stocks for their portfolios each year randomly. Assume you believe that all 1024 stock pickers are real financial managers who are carefully picking and choosing their ten stocks. You will be totally and utterly convinced that the stock picker with better than average investing results every year for ten straight years was a wunderkind. Ten consecutive years of better than average investing results sure looks like a great way to pick your financial advisor or financial manager.

In the real world, no one knows how many of the extraordinary investors you read about, are simply successful from lucky random chance than actual investing savvy. No way to know. That is the reason that persistence of investing performance is rare. If you insist on picking a financial advisor or financial manager, be careful. There really is no perfect method of selection. Remember from my chapter on the cost of investing, keeping costs as low as possible is important.

One last thought. If you have sufficient funds, diversify your funds between two or three financial managers or financial advisors. That way if one is particularly inept, unusually unlucky or corruptly fraudulent, you won't lose all off your investment assets.

## CHAPTER FOURTEEN:
# Retirement

What is Retirement?

Definition:
"Retirement is the withdrawal from one's position or occupation or from one's active working life. A person may also semi-retire by reducing work hours." (Wikipedia, September 21, 2020)

Our modern civilization with better food, better sanitation, the benefits of modern medicine and people's awareness of the need for improved personal care of their bodies has resulted in surprising (surprising at least to a person living in the 19th century) longer life expectancies. People may live thirty or more years after they stop full time work.

How do you obtain financial security if you may live thirty years after you retire?

How do you prepare for retirement?

How do you obtain income from your investments to fund your living expenses in your retirement years?

How much income is "safe" to withdraw and spend from your investments when you are in your retirement years?

From a financial point of view, Social Security payments provide enough money to keep you from flat out starving. Social security payments alone are not enough for you to do much more. Life is difficult when you cannot afford an unexpected $500 car repair. Life is more pleasant if you have an additional income stream to help pay for a nicer place to live, that unexpected car repair and the other things that make life more enjoyable.

How do you obtain that additional income stream?

Short of inheriting the money; short of winning the lottery; short of having a good traditional fully funded pension:

**FIRST: YOU NEED TO SAVE MONEY ON A REGULAR BASIS!**

**SECOND: YOU NEED TO GROW THAT MONEY WITH WISE LONG TERM INVESTING!**

I repeat:

**FIRST: YOU NEED TO SAVE MONEY ON A REGULAR BASIS!**

**SECOND: YOU NEED TO GROW THAT MONEY WITH WISE LONG TERM INVESTING!**

Building an income stream for the future requires that two things happen.

First, you need to actually save money.

That is, you need to put money aside. That is, you need the discipline to moderate your expenses throughout your life to have enough money left over each month or each year to actually save some of that money.

Second and equally important:

You need to invest that money in a way that will allow it to increase significantly in value over your working lifetime.

If you save $1000 each year and invest so that you earn on average 7% per year you will have approximately $108,000 after thirty years and $228,000 after forty years. Notice again, the huge difference between the thirty year result and the forty year result.

Following a similar calculation but in reverse, in order to have $1,000,000 after forty years you need to save and invest approximately $4,400 each year, if you invest and earn on average 7% per year. If you wanted $4,000,000 after forty years (assuming earning on average 7% per year) you would need to save approximately $17,500 each year.

All of you people out there earning $100,000, $200,000 a year or more, why aren't you saving more and investing it wisely?

How do you find the money to save?

How much do you need to save?

The answers to these two questions are different for everyone.

Let's look at the problem of saving and investing from the opposite point of view.

Question:

Following retirement, how much of your assets can you withdraw safely each year and not run out of money?

There is extensive discussion regarding what percentage of savings you can take out each year with reasonable confidence that you will not run out of money. Remember, nothing is completely safe. An often quoted rule is 4%. That is, you can withdraw up to 4% of your assets each year with a low probability of running out of money. This calculation is based on a portfolio of 50% stocks and 50% bonds. This calculation is based on the historical performance of stocks and bonds over the past hundred years or so. Recall, that trite saying, "Past performance is no guarantee of future performance." No one knows what the future performance of the stock market will be. No one knows what future inflation may be.

Some so called experts recommend withdrawing as much as 5% of total assets per year. Others recommend 3% of assets per year. I think the 4% per year recommendation is sensible with the caveat: You need to be prepared to lower your expenses if the economy hits a bad patch and your capital starts decreasing too fast. Alternatively, if the value of your assets in retirement increases more than expected you can always choose to increase your spending. Also, if you have serious health problems and a shortened life expectancy, increasing your spending for basic life support seems reasonable. Note: the 4% recommendation is just that, a recommendation. There is no way to prove its correctness. The 4% rule is an attempt to compromise between spending too little in your retirement and thereby not enjoying your retirement and spending too much and running out of money too soon.

So, back to the question: How to save?

If you work for a company that has a 401k plan or other retirement savings plan, you should maximize your contribution. The money placed in a 401K plan or similar plan is allowed by the government currently to grow tax free until it is withdrawn. Under current law it can be withdrawn after age 59 ½ without penalty. If possible, you should put off withdrawals until required by the "Required Minimum Distributions" mandated by the government. This allows your investments to continue to grow tax free for a longer period of time. After withdrawal you pay taxes as if the withdrawal is normal income under today's tax laws.

If your company has a matching program you definitely should maximize your contribution. The matching money is "found" money. The matching money is free money. That is, the matching money is money you "earn" by doing nothing more that contributing to your 401K. Likewise, if your company allows you to buy company stock at a discount, your company is giving you free money. Take it!

Under current law you need to actively choose to participate in the 401k saving plan of your company. You are not automatically enrolled. There is discussion regarding changing the law to make the enrollment automatic. As of this writing, this has not yet occurred. If you have a 401K and are not participating,

**ACT NOW; ACT TODAY**

**FULLY FUND YOUR 401K PLAN EVERY YEAR!**

Put yourself on automatic withdrawal from your paycheck and automatic deposit into your 401K account. This is part of playing games with yourself. If you don't see the money in your checking (spending) account you are less likely to spend it.

How much do you need to save? How do you develop the discipline to save? Easy questions. No clear answers. Certain questions need answering in this discussion. How old are you? The older you are the more you need to save because your investments have fewer years to grow.

Go back and read the chapter on exponential growth again. That will emphasize the importance of starting as early as you possibly can. Saving ten per cent of your income is certainly a good goal.

If you have to play games with yourself, do so. Set up an automatic transfer of money from your checking account to an investment account at a major financial firm. Set up automatic investing to transfer that money into a low cost United States stock index mutual fund. Make that money inviolate except for true family emergencies.

I currently use a credit card which pays back 2% on all charges on the card. You need to have an investment account at the financial firm which sponsors this credit card. There is no minimum amount to open the account. You can arrange for that 2% credit card refund to be automatically transferred to your investment account. Games you play with yourself. 2% of your credit card expenses are automatically invested in your investment account every month. You don't see the money, so you don't miss it. You don't see the money so you don't spend it.

If you set aside an inviolate investment account and program automatic transfers from your regular checking account to the investment account, you will just see the account balance in your checking (i.e. spending) account. Other games include buying a car and paying it off. After the car is paid off, continue paying off the car in a separate account. Keep your car ten years or more then buy the next one with cash. Cut down on your debts.

For your 401K recall the chapter on "yearly cost of investing." Put your 401K contributions into the lowest cost, all United States stock index mutual fund you are offered in your program.

Where and how should you invest your savings? Reread this book!!

How do you take income out of your retirement funds?

Most of my reading about taking income out of retirement funds discusses obtaining your income from interest from bonds and dividends from dividend paying stocks. This creates an automatic income stream. The average retiree is instructed to load up on bonds and dividend paying stocks to obtain the necessary income stream. I suppose if you are looking for the "simplest" approach which requires no thinking, then that is the way to go. Unfortunately, in today's ultra low interest rate environment, bonds are paying little. Currently, this approach generates a low income stream. I have expressed my opinion about the under pricing of bonds elsewhere in this book.

It is comfortable and comforting to have the income from bond interest and dividends automatically appear in your investment account and then be automatically transferred to your checking account. You don't have to do anything. You don't have to think.

As previously discussed, bonds do not provide the growth of capital needed for any period of time greater than ten years. If you retire at 60 years of age and may live to 90 or older, you have a time horizon of as much as thirty years or more.

During retirement, how much money should you keep as cash or cash-like investments including money market mutual funds, certificates of deposit and short-term bond funds?

There is no absolute, correct answer to this question. There is a general principle often quoted that any money you are going to need within the next five years should not be invested in stocks or other volatile (volatile in the short term) investments. The reason? You may hit a five year downturn in the stock market and have to sell investments when their value has dropped.

My personal preference is to keep a five to seven year amount of your anticipated income withdrawals in cash-like investments, namely money market mutual funds, certificates of deposit and short term bond funds. I replenish each year's cash withdrawal with the sale of stock mutual fund shares. With a five to seven year cushion of "cash", if the market drops precipitously you are not forced to sell investments which are at a low point to obtain income. If the market is down you do not replenish your five to seven year cash cushion. You wait until the market recovers. You can wait until the market recovers to replenish your cash like reserve. You have the cash like investments to use and are able to wait five to seven years for the market to recover. I repeat: if the market is way down, you don't replenish the cash reserve until the market recovers. I would keep the rest of your assets in low cost United States index stock mutual funds.

With five or seven years of needed income ready in cash-like investments, psychologically you should be able to ignore the occasional wild swings in the stock market.

Why?

You have five or seven years of cash available and do not need to respond to stock market swings for five or seven years.

If the market is not depressed then each year you sell sufficient shares in your low cost index stock mutual funds to give you the replacement for the five or seven year cash like investment amount you need. Thus, you arrange to sell shares of the low-cost stock index fund whenever you need to replenish the five or seven year stash of cash-like assets. You can arrange to automatically sell a certain amount of your low cost index stock fund every month to replenish that month's income. If you are taking Required Minimum Distributions you can keep some of the reserve cash-like investments in your IRA and fund part of your living expenses from the IRA Required Minimum Distributions.

When selling mutual fund or ETF shares to fund your retirement, you want to sell the shares of the mutual fund which will result in the lowest amount of tax you need to pay on your capital gains. For assets in IRAs, Roll-Over IRAs and 401Ks, at present time, there is no tax consequence for selling assets at this time. You are only taxed for withdrawals. Tax laws always change. Learn what the tax laws are now!

If you have assets in a 401k or IRA after you turn 72, you are required to begin taking out your required minimum distribution. You are allowed to take that distribution out in cash or using an in-kind distribution in which you transfer shares of the stock or mutual fund and document the value on the day of distribution. These rules may change. Tax laws change frequently. Learn what the tax laws are now!

Learn the current tax laws!

Remember to take out your required minimum distribution each year! (If you are old enough)

Remember to pay the estimated income tax owed after you have taken out that distribution!

The 401K programs of most companies are expensive. That is, the yearly fees of the financial firms running the 401k program are more than 0.5% and often much higher. Then the fee of the mutual fund you are allowed to invest in often brings your yearly fee over 1%. This severely affects your eventual retirement fund value. Put your money in the least expensive stock index fund in your plan! When you retire or change jobs transfer your money to a rollover IRA account at a large financial firm and switch to low cost United States all stock index funds. When you reach the age at which you are allowed to transfer money out of your 401k plan, do so. Transfer to a rollover IRA. That way you decrease the yearly cost of your investing that money.

CEOs take note! Can you find a better way to run your company's retirement plan with lower costs? The costs are eating up your own investment performance too!

Costs matter! Costs matter! Costs matter!

I repeat:

Find out the age at which you are allowed to withdraw your assets from the retirement fund without penalty. When you reach that age transfer the money to a rollover IRA which you open at a financial firm and invest in low cost all United States stock index funds. Then each year as money is deposited into your company retirement fund, transfer it to your rollover IRA so that your yearly fees are minimized. Similarly, if you change jobs transfer your 401k money to a rollover IRA so that you can minimize your yearly investment costs.

Do not, do not, do not transfer the money to a non-IRA account even temporarily!

That will count as a distribution and cost you heavily tax-wise. Open your roll-over IRA account first and check, double check and triple check that you are transferring the assets correctly.

In retirement you will have serious concerns regarding your risk of outliving, i.e. outspending, your assets and living the rest of your life pauperized. The flip side of this, is the fact that if you are too conservative regarding your spending you will spend the rest of your life enjoying it less than you might otherwise.

I have recommended avoiding the high yearly cost of financial advisors, financial managers, registered investment advisors, hedge fund managers, etc. So, where should you get advice. Accountants can give you advice regarding your tax related questions at a one time meeting with follow up phone calls, emails or meetings as needed. An estate attorney can give advice regarding your estate and wills. You pay for the will preparation one time and then additional time and advice as needed.

You don't pay a yearly percentage of your net worth to anyone.

Regarding the question of where to invest your money: Read this book again!

# CHAPTER FIFTEEN:
# Predicting the Future

"Prediction is difficult; especially when it concerns the future"

NB: My online search indicates that there are many versions of this statement and that the origin of this saying is murky.

## CHAPTER SIXTEEN:
# Further Discussion Regarding Predicting the Future

---

Trying to predict the future is a fool's game.

That doesn't mean we don't try.

Consider:

There exist fifty and one-hundred-year bonds put out by both companies and countries and purchased by individuals, mutual funds and/or financial advisors and financial managers. This means that investors are loaning money to companies and/or countries for fifty to one hundred years.

STOP!

Think for a while.

Do you think investing in a fifty or one-hundred-year bond is a good investment?

If your answer is yes. Why is your answer yes?

If your answer is no. Why is your answer no?

Think about this for a while before going on to the next page.

Welcome back!

Anyone buying a fifty-year bond or a one-hundred-year bond is predicting a calm, unsullied, minimally changing future extending out fifty to one-hundred years. When has that ever, and I mean ever, happened? Interest rates are currently near all time lows and have been that way for a number of years. The purchasers of these fifty and one hundred years bonds are predicting that interest rates will remain stable and low for the next fifty to one hundred years.

Wow! Takes my breath away. Remember my earlier comments about the under pricing of bonds.

These bond purchasers are forgetting the inflation which accompanied World War I and World War II. These bond purchasers are forgetting the inflation of the late 1970s and early 1980s. These bond purchasers are forgetting that the current low levels of inflation and the current low interest rates are an historic anachronism and not the long term norm.

There is a tendency among many people to assume and predict that current short term trends indicate long term trends.

This is called the "**fallacy of extrapolation**."

There is another concept, I wish to discuss, called "**regression to the mean**."

Definition:
"In statistics, regression towards the mean or (regression to the mean) is the phenomenon that arises if a sample point of a random variable is extreme (nearly an outlier), a future point will be closer to the mean or average on further measurements." (Wikipedia, October 16, 2020)

Personally, I would amend that definition. That definition should contain the statement that a future point will most likely be closer to the mean. There is always a small chance a single future point will also be that extreme or even more extreme. Also, ignore the convoluted words of that definition and read the next paragraph.

Stated more simply, regression towards the mean means that when "something" has gone to an extreme, (think an unusually great golf game, an unusual run of good or bad luck gambling, unusually high or low interest rates, an unusually high or low grade on a test at school, etc.) then there is high probability that the following "something" will likely be closer to whatever they usually are (think an average golf game, average luck gambling, average interest rates, average grade on a test, etc.)

Baring major changes in the world, the same is true of the stock market. If the stock market goes through a period of low volatility for a period of time, it will probably become more volatile in the future due to regression to the mean. Similarly, if the stock market is more volatile than usual for a period of time, it will probably become less volatile in time through regression to the mean.

Similarly, if the stock market rises or falls unusually quickly, this probably will not continue long term, again through regression to the mean. The stock market, as a whole, increases on average every year. Regression to the mean for the stock market means regression to the average increase over time.

This, of course, may not (will not) last forever. Permanent changes in life, the universe and everything may occur which permanently change the "mean" of whatever you are measuring.

The day World War I ended, few people, if any, predicted World War II. The day World War I ended there may have been a few nuclear physicists who recognized that the energy contained within the atom might result in a massive bomb. However, that was not common knowledge.

Given a fifty year investment horizon what might happen within that time span?

Answer:

Pretty much anything.

This uncertainty involves both good uncertainty and bad uncertainty along a continuous spectrum. The world may enter a long period of spectacular prosperity with increasing productivity, personal freedom and increasing standard of living for most of the inhabitants of our precious Earth. Might happen. Hope it happens. Is it a chancy prediction? Oh, Yes! Whether this will happen is definitely uncertain.

What are some of the uncertain bad outcomes? China is currently a dictatorship run by one man. There may be instability when he no longer rules China and possibly before. How bad will the instability be? Following the one family: one child policy, China is entering a period of a decreasing fraction of the population being of a working age. This may lead to an economic downturn in China and may be another cause of instability in China. In China and India men outnumber women on a massive scale. This imbalance may be a source of societal instability. There is always the risk of miscalculation and war with Taiwan or India. Similarly, in Russia there may be instability when the current leader no longer rules and possibly before. The result of this instability is, of course, unpredictable.

What about the Middle East? The continuing strife between the Sunni and Shia will probably lead to instability that might take many turns that are completely unpredictable. The continuing strife between the Arabs and the Israelis also leads to unpredictability. The new Abraham Accords raise some hope for increasing peace. However, the continued strength of Islamic terrorists and the actions of the ruling mullahs of Iran continue to cause concern for stability in the Middle East.

I have just rewritten this sentence on November 12, 2020. Biden has won the presidential election.

Let me ask a question.

Does the result of this presidential election allow you, me or anyone to predict where the stock market will be in ten years, in twenty years or in fifty years?

The correct answer obviously is "NO!"

With all of the seesawing back and forth between the two political parties, can anyone predict where the United States will be politically in twenty years?

The correct answer obviously is "NO!"

With a twenty to fifty year investment time horizon, should I alter my investment allocations after reading today's news?

To me, the correct answer obviously is "NO!"

I am unable to predict where we will be in twenty years. Any decision to change my investment allocations due to anything happening in this election while operating with a twenty to fifty year time horizon is pure fancy, pure folly, pure nonsense.

In the United States the increasing strife between the Left and the Right, between the Progressives and the Conservatives may take unpredictable turns. The fact that the two sides: 1. Do not talk to each other, 2. Lie about each other, 3. Rarely cooperate with each other, and 4. Rarely compromise with each other leads to serious uncertainty regarding the future of the United States.

For the moment, the United States remains the bastion of freedom and stability in the world. For this reason, the dollar is considered the safest currency in the world. I think that the reason interest rates have stayed low for so long is that many people around the world are most comfortable holding their assets in United States government dollar denominated bonds. This is felt to be the safest investment by many. As I have stated before, this also leads to the under pricing of United States bonds.

Is New Zealand safe? New Zealand is safe under the umbrella of the Pax Americana. The United States would not tolerate an invasion of New Zealand. If the Pax Americana falters then New Zealand no longer seems so safe.

I have discussed previously my recommendation toward long term use of low cost United States stock index mutual funds for the average investor. What are some of the long term negative risks of this advice?

The S&P 500 stock index follows the valuation of the 500 largest corporations in the United States. "The average annual total return and compound annual growth rate of the index including dividends, since its inception in 1926 has been approximately 9.8% or 6% after inflation." (Wikipedia, 8/17/20) Other sources state that total value of the stock market in the United States over the last one hundred and twenty years or so has on average risen approximately 7% in value per year.

Why?

Why has the total value of stocks in the stock markets of the United States increased at least an average of 7% per year over an extended period of time in the United States?

Why?

This has not happened in every country. Japan, for example, has endured an extended period of a relatively flat stock market lasting decades.

I have not seen this question asked and answered in my reading up to this time.

I do not think anyone knows the answer with any confidence. I have asked numerous financial advisors that question. I have never received an answer. My best guess is that there are several reasons. The first is population growth through birth rate and immigration of young people increasing the number of productive members of society. The second is increased productivity through increased efficiency and technology. Advances in technology have added entire new forms of consumption. The third is the fact that we live in a relatively stable society.

What are the general criteria necessary for long term economic advancement in a country? You need a society which has acceptable political stability long term. I think this is found in democratic countries in which the benefits of the economy are dispersed more evenly than most other countries. You need the rule of law. You have to know that if you buy property and improve that property you will be allowed to keep it and not have it stolen. You need to know that you will be able to benefit your children with the results of your efforts. You need a country whose population continues to grow through birth rate and/or immigration of young people. Countries with these properties are more likely to remain stable long term. Basically, you need a country with a market capitalism type of society.

Autocratic countries, such as the China, Russia and Iran of 2020, are more likely to be unstable in the long term. A country like Japan which has had a low birth rate and low immigration for years is less likely to experience prolonged economic expansion. The old saw, "Nothing lasts forever" is utterly true. Even stable countries can change over the long term. Nothing prevents a culture or a country from committing suicide from unrest and/or changes in basic values. The community of Shakers is an archetypal example of a culture committing suicide. The Shakers practiced celibacy. With no new births to expand their population, they died out from too few recruits.

Trying to predict technological changes in the future is truly impossible. I assume that advances in artificial intelligence will reach a point in which there will be significantly less need or opportunity for unskilled workers. Will this lead to economic and social instability? A true unknown. The possibility for nuclear war or a manmade biological epidemic exists. Dystopic future literature is filled with possibilities thought of by people much more creative than I.

Considering long term investing, you have to assume that civilization as we know it will continue in some recognizable form. Trying to pick the winners and losers in individual stocks is probably impossible for the average passive investor.

For the near future, investing in low cost United States stock index mutual funds is probably the "easiest" and "safest" approach for most ordinary folks like myself and like you. You can diversify into several different low cost United States stock index funds.

One fatal flaw of democracy may be the continual promise by politicians of more goodies than they are willing or able to pay for. By pay for I mean tax for. If the national debt continues to balloon, the government will end up printing more money to pay for the debt. The US government can't go bankrupt because it can always print more money. States and cities can go bankrupt. They can't print money. Printing excessive amounts of money results in the money being worth less. That is called inflation which I discussed earlier. I assume that the rate of inflation in the United States will increase at some unknown time in the future. If there comes a time when the United States is no longer viewed as a bastion of stability, the United States will no longer be able to fund its increasing debt cheaply. It will pay the interest on its debt with cheaper money via inflation. This may lead to social instability.

There was marked inflation during World War One. My grandmother became a widow in her 40s. All of her assets were invested in "safe" bonds. Following the inflation which accompanied World War I in the United States, my grandmother's "financial security" was no longer "secure." Because all of her assets were invested in "safe" bonds, her remaining assets did not grow. She later ran out of money and was supported by my parents. I have seen how inflation pauperized my grandmother. I have seen how "safe" investing pauperized my grandmother.

History is replete with stories of civilizations which ascended and later fell. The future of the United States and the world is unknowable. If the United States descends into deterioration and decay from societal ills it is unable or unwilling to repair, then emigrating to a better place is an option. After all, all of us are immigrants or descendants of immigrants who were seeking a better place. When I say all of us, I mean all of us. Even the indigenous American Indians are the descendants of immigrants who came over from Asia tens of thousands of years ago seeking a better life.

Hopefully, the American dream of a vibrant, equal, economically successful, mutual enterprise will continue indefinitely. Saving and investing for the future long term will allow you to enjoy this success.

# CHAPTER SEVENTEEN:
## Reprise

1. Modern Portfolio Theory defines the investment risk of a basket of assets as the standard deviation of the day to day volatility of the combined value of that basket of assets.
2. I argue that the day to day volatility of the combined value of a basket of assets is a short term phenomenon has little to no correlation with the value of that basket of assets in five, ten, twenty or fifty years in the future. You should not be investing in non-cash assets if your time horizon is less than five to seven years. I argue that the day to day volatility of a basket of assets is not a valid risk measure for investments greater than five or more years. I argue that the day to day volatility of a basket of assets is not a valid measure of investment risk for any reasonable investment time horizon.
3. Emphasis on reducing the day to day volatility of your basket of assets leads to excessive diversification.
4. Excessive diversification leads to investing in lower performing assets.
5. Due to their perceived "safety" (at this time) bonds are under priced and are lower performing assets.

6. Most financial advisors and financial managers emphasize the need for extensive diversification. This makes investing seem too complicated for the average investor to do on his or her own. The extensive diversification minimizes the day to day volatility in the value of the basket of assets. Thus, in a major stock market downturn the value of the basket of assets will drop less in the short term and the average investor will be less likely to withdraw his or her assets from the financial advisor or financial manager.

7. The cost of investing is a major factor in the final value of an investor's assets following long term horizon investing. Keeping costs down is key! This involves ditching financial advisors and financial managers who charge a percentage of the total value invested each year. Keeping investing costs down also involves ditching financial managers who charge a significant percentage of profits made from your investments.

8. Looking back over one hundred years, stocks, as a whole, have outperformed bonds for almost all ten-year time periods. Stocks have outperformed bonds for ALL twenty-year time periods and longer time periods over the past one hundred years.

9. Low-cost United States stock index mutual funds, held in a buy and hold strategy, for long term time horizons provide the best chance of the best investing results going forward for the average, passive investor. This provides adequate diversification. This does not require rebalancing.

10. Small capitalization stocks and value stocks have outperformed large cap and growth cap stocks over twenty year time horizons. Thus, weighting toward small cap and value stocks for the long term is sensible.

11. A long term buy and hold in United States stock index mutual funds strategy is not exciting. The benefits are not seen immediately. Only with time does the exponential growth of a long term buy and hold with stock index mutual funds strategy begin to manifest itself. Only with time do the outstanding investing results become evident.

12. I am not the only one writing about long term buy and hold strategies, keeping down the cost of investing, not panicking when the market

tanks, etc. Warren Buffet is an American investor, business tycoon and chairman of Berkshire Hathaway, Inc. He is considered one of the most successful investors in the world. (Wikipedia, November 13, 2020) Here are some quotes from the 2013 Shareholder letter of Berkshire Hathaway Inc. written by Warren Buffet

a. "You don't need to be an expert in order to achieve satisfactory investment returns. But if you aren't, you must recognize your limitations and follow a course certain to work reasonably well. Keep things simple and don't swing for the fences. When promised quick profits, respond with a quick "no.""

b. "Owners of stocks, however, too often let the capricious and often irrational behavior of their fellow owners cause them to behave irrationally as well. Because there is so much chatter about markets, the economy, interest rates, price behavior of stocks, etc., some investors believe it is important to listen to pundits – and, worse yet, important to consider acting upon their comments."

c. "I have good news for these non-professionals: The typical investor doesn't need this skill. In aggregate, American business has done wonderfully over time and will continue to do so (though, most assuredly, in unpredictable fits and starts). In the 20th Century, the Dow Jones Industrials index advanced from 66 to 11,497, paying a rising stream of dividends to boot. The 21st Century will witness further gains, almost certain to be substantial. The goal of the non-professional should not be to pick winners – neither he nor his "helpers" can do that – but should rather be to own a cross-section of businesses that in aggregate are bound to do well. A low-cost S&P 500 index fund will achieve this goal."

d. "That's the "what" of investing for the non-professional. The "when" is also important. The main danger is that the timid or beginning investor will enter the market at a time of extreme exuberance and then become disillusioned when paper losses occur. ….. The antidote to that kind of mistiming is for an investor to accumulate shares over a long period and never to sell when the news is bad and stocks are well off their highs. Following those rules, the "know-nothing" investor who both diversifies and keeps his costs minimal is virtually certain to get satisfactory results. Indeed, the unsophisticated investor who is realistic about his shortcomings is likely to obtain better long-term results than the knowledgeable professional who is blind to even a single weakness."

# CHAPTER EIGHTEEN:
# Precis

Investing good: gambling bad

Saving good: over spending bad

Investing costs low good: investing costs high bad

Long term buy and hold good: frequent buys and sells bad

Make your own decisions good: totally rely on financial advisors/managers bad

Moderate diversification good: over diversification bad

Buy and hold good: too much rebalancing bad

Moderate self-confidence good: over confidence and under confidence bad

Pay with cash good: too much debt bad

Long term buy and hold in low cost stock index funds good: day trading bad

Following my advice good: ignoring my advice bad

CHAPTER NINETEEN:
# The End: The Conclusion; The Summation: Finis

Becoming financially literate is important for everyone. Becoming financially comfortable requires discipline with respect to working and saving. Becoming financially comfortable requires avoiding overspending and overborrowing. Becoming financially comfortable requires wise investing. How to invest wisely and successfully unfortunately is not common knowledge. By dealing with the issue of how to invest, I hope I have contributed to general financial literacy by writing this book.

A key concept is that your financial advisor or financial manager is strictly speaking "not your friend." Your financial advisor or financial manager "manages" to make an excellent hourly income from managing you and your assets. The owners of the large hedge funds are often billionaires. How did they amass so much money? From fees earned while managing other people's assets!

In this book I have attempted to highlight certain requirements for successful long term investing. These include discipline with respect to spending and saving, attention to minimizing the "cost" of your investing behavior and determining your proper level and type of diversification. Successful long term investing avoids the expensive use of financial managers and financial advisors.

I am not the only one writing that the cost of investing is one of the biggest determinants of the long term results of investing. As I emphasize in my book, the yearly cost of investing "compounds" over time. The yearly cost of investing is the exact opposite of exponential growth. The yearly cost of investing is, in essence, "exponential loss." How do you minimize the cost of investing? Become your own "teacher." Stop paying "high" fees!!!!!

In this book, I have challenged the current hegemony of belief in the religion of The Modern Portfolio Theory. I have challenged the basic assumption that the volatility of the day to day value of your basket of assets is a valid measure of risk, particularly if you are investing for multiple decades in a buy and hold strategy in low cost all United States stock index funds (mutual or ETF).

In this book I have challenged the use of the extensive diversification that leads to investments in poor performing assets. The use of extensive diversification leads to lower long term investment results because of the use of these lower performing investments. The use of extensive diversification makes simple, ordinary investing seem too complicated, thus leading to you feeling a need for a costly financial manager or financial advisor.

Is my challenge to the Modern Portfolio Theory truth? Am I spouting hot air? Am I guilty of hubris in my own belief? To echo a news organization: "I report; you decide". If you decide that I make sense, your conclusion should lead you to significant changes in your investing behavior.

You want to control the "known" risks. These are not the issues normally associated with the word "risk." Yet, these investing behaviors are the most "risky" risks, in that these investing behaviors are most likely to result in significantly poorer investment performance long term. These "risky" risks include unnecessary high yearly cost of investing, exhilaration and fear which result in buying high and selling low, trying to time the stock market, fraud and your own hubris and overconfidence. The other, perhaps, "riskiest" risk is panic selling when the stock market tanks.

As I have stated earlier. There are unknown risks out there. Like looking at an old map and seeing an area marked, "Here be monsters." These unknown risks include black swan pandemics, bioterror, the four horsemen of death, famine, war and conquest, social unrest, cultural suicide, political societal upheaval and possible dystopic futures of infinite varieties. There are societal upheavals sufficiently severe that no amount of planning can protect against them. You, the reader, need to accept this, ignore this as much as is humanly possible and get on with your life.

Investing, particularly investing for the long term, requires an optimistic approach to life. Live your life to the fullest. Plan for your best possible future. Save and invest wisely! Live! Love! Prosper! God Spede!!

Note: Spede is the olde, obsolete English spelling.